MODI'S

MISSION

MODI'S

MISSION

BERJIS DESAI

RUPA

Published by
Rupa Publications India Pvt. Ltd 2025
161-B/4, Gulmohar House,
Yusuf Sarai Community Centre,
New Delhi 110049

Sales centres:
Bengaluru Chennai
Hyderabad Kolkata Mumbai

The views and opinions expressed in this book are the author's own and the facts are as reported by him, which have been verified to the extent possible, and the publishers are not in any way liable for the same.

P-ISBN: 978-93-7003-340-5
E-ISBN: 978-93-7003-244-6

First impression 2025

10 9 8 7 6 5 4 3 2 1

Printed in India

To

all those

who transformed India from a country to a Nation

Contents

Author's Note

Fifty years later, Modi and Gandhi will be mentioned in the same breath and the same order.

It is a fallacy to think that Modi is just another politician. In the history of every great nation, and in every century or so, a leader is born with a mission. His primary task is to raise the collective consciousness of the people. It was Gandhi in the 20th century; it is Modi in the 21st.

The central thesis of this work is that Narendra Modi is a high energy with an entrusted mission to set India on the path to its destined glory.

Modi's journey though outwardly political conceals the unfolding of relentless energy in ensuring that India reaches its profound national destiny. Modi somewhat reluctantly donned the role of a politician. He was on the verge of becoming a renunciate when a higher calling from the forces that govern India's destiny revealed that his true purpose in this lifetime was to serve and lead the nation.

What exactly is meant by the forces that govern India's destiny? Rabindranath Tagore, a Nobel laureate poet, composed a hymn in Bengali in 1911, called *Bharoto Bhagyo Bidhata*, whose first stanza was anointed in January 1950 by the Constituent Assembly, as India's national anthem. Tagore translated: *Jana Gana Mana, Adhinayaka Jaya He! Bharata Bhagya Vidhata,* in English, as: O Ruler of the minds of the people! Victory be to you, O Dispenser of the Destiny of India! Sri Aurobindo, the sage of Puducherry (Pondicherry), and the outstanding intellectual mystic of the 20th century, echoed Tagore by writing: The Shakti we call Bhawani Bharati is the living unity of all the Shaktis.

Bharat Bhagya Vidhata or Bhawani Bharati, the idea of the Indian Nation, as a vibrant living entity, has begun to resonate with millions of Indians.

After Independence, over time, a cynical acceptance of the substandard and the mediocre had set in. The people were in a kind of daze or stupor. The Nation's karma demanded a catalyst to radically change the thinking of the people. Narendra Modi is that catalyst. Ultimately, Modi's task is to pull millions out of poverty, both of body and mind, by giant strides into building physical and socioeconomic infrastructure, which necessarily involves bulldozing institutional insularity to reform. More importantly, by making Indians believe that what is happening around them is real change and things will no longer meander lazily as before. This requires an assertion of national identity. A nation is what a nation believes. At a deeper level, Indians had to be made conscious of their unparalleled cultural heritage.

An indolent Hinduism, not as a religion but as a way of life, had to be galvanized to secure national boundaries against physical, economic and psychological invasion. In the process, effective communication with the people may appear, at times, to be strident. A near-untranslatable Sanskrit word, *asmita*, the realization of being, has to flower. The truth is that without Hinduism as an all-encompassing civilizational and cultural idea, India cannot become a superpower, which is her inexorable destiny. Modi is the first of the instruments for fulfilling this destiny.

Modi could not have achieved so many near-impossible goals in a quarter of a century if he had not been so guided. Raising the consciousness of 1.4 billion people is a Herculean task. Throughout his career, Modi has had to overcome roadblocks created at every step to prevent him from gaining power including investigations to disqualify him from public office. This included not only political opponents but also some of his own party men. Without a single exception, he has overcome every insurmountable obstacle. His success is due to his tenacity, fearlessness, and like a consummate chess player, his ability to think ten steps ahead; blessed that he is by the forces that safeguard him. In an assignment of this nature, the means occasionally seem unorthodox. This irks a section of the intellectual elite to no end.

The thinking of this elite is straitjacketed by Western paradigms. Mindlessly aping political correctness has vitiated our unique national story. Our sociopolitical language and definitions require to be restated to suit the nation's narrative. Intellectual dialogue in India has become hollow, puerile and predictable. It is out of sync with the ground realities and the aspirations of the people. Even those of the elite who are convinced that Modi is exactly what India requires, lack the courage to voice their views. It has become fashionable for the elite to be anti-Modi. Just as it is fashionable to be allergic to Hinduism. This includes some historians and commentators who negate or sterilize history, a pernicious exercise. Unwittingly or otherwise, this elite has become a tool in the hands of inimical foreign powers and the cynical Western media to downsize India.

Until Modi became Prime Minister, the influential in both the financial and political capitals of India sustained mutually exploitative ties with political leaders. None has the temerity to do so with Modi. This lack of special treatment makes Lutyen's Delhi angry, frustrated and humiliated. Modi has to tolerate them at times in the larger interests of the economy and the country. Capitalists are not his cronies, as alleged by his opponents; they are the tools and medium for growth. On the other hand, an overwhelming majority instinctively believes and trusts in Modi to do what is the greatest good of the greatest number. Even on a mundane level, his electoral success is attributable to this simple arithmetic.

Modi knows what it entails to be thankful for every meal and the thrill of wearing a new shirt. However, his compassion for the suffering is not attributable to his personal experience alone. It spontaneously arises from an inner realization of his mission. Modi, a spiritually conscious being, with a yogic past, dispassionately performs the functions of a ruler. His detractors realize that they cannot assail his personal integrity which like Caesar's wife, is beyond suspicion. They also grudgingly acknowledge his stellar administrative acumen, his relentless hard work, the purity of his patriotism, his foresight and strategy. So, they dub him authoritarian and communalist. They call him a Hindu fanatic who is tearing apart the secular fabric of the Republic. This book demonstrates the hollowness of these allegations.

This book is not a biography. Neither is it a hagiography. A hagiography involves undue reverence for its subject. Spontaneous reverence there may be, however, it is due and deserved. In any event, Narendra Modi requires no hagiography.

This work is more about Narendra Modi as an idea, a movement, an instrument of change. It is about the transformation he has brought about in the collective consciousness of Indians. It examines Modi's life mission from this unique perspective. Hopefully, it will convince a dispassionate reader to appreciate the reality underlying Modi. The constant undermining of his extraordinary achievements by the Western media, and the angst of a section of the Indian intellectual elite against him, needs to be dispelled. This analysis is inspired by this sole objective.

▪

In September 2007, the World Economic Forum had organized the inaugural 'Summer Davos' in Dalian in China. I was attending the event as a delegate of an Indian corporate providing technology to manufacture biofuels. I was waiting in the foyer of the hotel at dinner time, when a Secretary of the Government of Gujarat, which had set up a pavilion at the event, walked up to me and said, '*Saheb* is standing alone. Would you mind talking to him for five minutes?' Narendra

Modi looked at my nameplate, smiled, and said in Gujarati, 'Desai. Parsi from Navsari?' I vigorously nodded. Modi rattled off a dozen details about the Parsi priestly class in Navsari and asked, 'Aren't you an ordained Zoroastrian priest?' I was amazed at how he had fathomed. He handed me his visiting card in English and in Chinese on the reverse, saying 'CEO, Gujarat, India.' Suddenly, I wanted to tell him that one day he would be India's Prime Minister. Before I could, he was surrounded by many others. I hesitated and left. I had not an iota of doubt that my intuition would come true.

▪

This writer, now a near-retired lawyer with 45 years of practice, belongs to the micro-minority Parsi Zoroastrian community and is a practicing Zoroastrian. This writer has never had any link or affiliation with any political party or any governmental or public body. Nor has he ever held any public or political post or position.

Berjis Desai
Mumbai
2nd August 2025

Prologue

'Shri Narendra Damodardas Modi, Prime Minister of India', announced the secretary to President Pranab Mukherjee, followed by a long applause in the forecourt of the Rashtrapati Bhavan. The President of India, Pranab Mukherjee, sat still, his expression unreadable, as history turned another page before him. For years, despite his stature, his party had never chosen him for the prime minister's chair—a decision that had shaped the course of Congress politics. Sonia Gandhi, the Congress president, whose choice had elevated Manmohan Singh to the nation's highest office, remained a quiet presence in the backdrop of power. And there was Manmohan Singh—the scholar-prime minister—watching the proceedings with his head slightly inclined, his famously impassive face betraying nothing as he silently witnessed the transfer of power.

Modi, dressed in a crisp cream coloured kurta and churidar and a brownish *bandi*, strode up to the dais thinking only of Ganesha, the elephant-headed God of all auspicious beginnings and remover of all obstacles, who had appeared regularly in his dreams since he was four. Sometimes benignly smiling, sometimes violently dancing; always protective and guarding. *Om Gan Ganpataye Namah*, he intoned and took three deep breaths as he always does at crucial moments in life.

'I, Narendra Damodardas Modi,' he began his oath, in chaste Hindi, without a trace of his native Gujarati accent, do swear in the name of God, 'that I shall always uphold the sovereignty and integrity of India.' As his stentorian voice boomed, the politicians, civil servants and business heads gathered there instinctively knew that India would never be the same again.

Vadnagar was bursting with pride and joy at the fairy tale ascent of its son to the pinnacle of power. Earlier, its inhabitants had watched with a sense of near disbelief when he had unexpectedly been sworn in as the Chief Minister of Gujarat state in October 2001, and then thrice in succession, in 2002, 2007 and 2012. And today, on 26 May 2014, the ancient town gave India its first prime minister born after Independence.

Modi's mission had begun.

CHAPTER ONE

No Harrow, No Oxbridge

ON 17TH SEPTEMBER 1950, when Narendra was delivered by a mid-wife at home, Vadnagar was a tiny town in the Mehsana district of the then State of Bombay, blissfully unaware of its unique heritage. Twenty kilometres away, were the Taranga Hills, sacred to both Jains and Buddhists.

When Narendra was five, braving the sweltering 46° C, he loitered alongside his two elder brothers through the labyrinthine *mohallas* and was fascinated to see a lot of digging near the eastern bank of Sharmistha Lake. He was unaware that Vadnagar was on the cusp of becoming famous.

Findings of red polished ware, led the University of Baroda, enjoying the patronage of Maharaja Siyajirao Gaekwad III, to excavate and discover the existence of three distinct cultures-Hindu, Buddhist and Jain-dating from 100 CE up to 1000 CE. Excavations continued sporadically, until in 2024, it was conclusively proved that Vadnagar had been in continuous, uninterrupted human occupation for more than 2700 years, making it one of the oldest living towns in

India.[1] A post-Harappan urban hub going all the way back to 800 BCE.[2] Here, Buddhist monasteries had thrived; Jain holy sutras were recited for the first time in public; ancient Shiv and Shakti temples abounded. A melting pot of socioreligious and cultural milieu was Vadnagar. Many spiritually advanced souls had lived, died and perhaps reincarnated here. Devotional fervour poured over millennia had made this land spiritually vibrant.

Its past may have been glorious; however, three years after Independence, it appeared to be in survival mode. While agriculture and animal husbandry were the mainstay of the Vadnagar economy, minor traders and service providers were struggling to survive. The *Modi Ghanchi* community, to which Modi belonged, got its name from its occupation of being oil pressers. Traditionally, cold pressing oilseeds to produce unrefined edible oil was an integral part of the agrarian economy, with the oil cakes fed to the cattle. In 1937, Lever Brothers launched *vanaspati* or hydrogenated refined edible oil for the first time in India, under the brand name Dalda, followed by a host of other manufacturers, virtually destroying the oil pressing cottage industry.

■

---

1. Ghosh, Bishwanath. 'India's Oldest Living City Found in PM Modi's Native Village Vadnagar: Multi-Institution Study', *The Hindu*, 13 January 2024, https://tinyurl.com/4dhfpy4m. Accessed on 10 September 2025.
2 'Vadnagar—A Multi-Layered Historic Town, Gujarat.' *UNESCO World Heritage Centre*, 13 December 2022, https://tinyurl. com/3satwdpz. Accessed on 10 September.

Damodardas, Narendra's father, left home every single day at 4 a.m., stopped to pray at the local temple, before opening his little tea shop at the Vadnagar railway station, which had flagged its first train on the Mehsana—Taranga line on 21st March 1887. Neighbours would know from his heavy footsteps on the cobbled pathway that it must be 4 a.m.

Most *mohalla*s of Vadnagar comprised of a narrow cobblestoned pathway sandwiched on either side by a row of houses, stuck to each other like unwilling Siamese twins, constructed out of local wood, hardened mud, stone and bricks. The *mohalla* often shared a well, the only source of drinking cooking and washing water, with a tortoise lowered in it to act as a natural germicide and for being auspicious. The well was holy, pure and an object of worship. Ghee lamps were lit near the well and it was garlanded with marigold flowers. The other shared facility was the makeshift latrine system.

The toilet was an open-air affair in the distant fields for both sexes. In a few homes, where there was a toilet, one sat on the haunches over a two-foot hole in the ground, and the waste was collected in a straw basket. All the latrines in a *mohalla* were synchronized to ensure that the straw baskets were placed more or less in a row in a pathway running behind the houses, which a service worker accessed twice a day. She announced her presence loudly before picking up the basket, emptying its contents and replacing it, to warn anyone using the system to suspend the ongoing process. Vadnagar had watched with wide-eyed wonder when the thunder water closets (pulling a chain on a wall-mounted flush tank) were first introduced in Gujarat in the early 1970s. A self-cleaning toilet at home felt like heaven. Decades later, as Prime Minister, Modi's government would create 12 crores toilets and take steps to restore the dignity of sanitation workers—*swachhata ke sainik* (soldiers of cleanliness) as Modi calls them. Manual scavenging was declared a moral blight by Modi, who has consistently worked towards ending it completely.

In one such house, with inadequate ventilation and no windows or main door to speak of, Narendra stayed with his parents and five siblings as also a cow which provided milk to the family, as also for the tea business of his father. Heeraba, his mother, supplemented the family's meagre income by washing utensils at a few houses, Modi had written in a blog on her turning 99 years of age.[3]

Although Gujarat became the first state in India in 2006 to electrify all its villages,[4] when Narendra was born, Vadnagar homes had no electricity. Flat-wick lamps burning kerosene, provided dim light. Kerosene irritated the eyes and throat. Narendra remembers cleaning, along with his brothers, the glass chimney getting fogged. Several years later, when Vadnagar finally did receive electricity, the power supply stuttered and was erratic with almost daily outages. Modi's house though had no electricity when he left home permanently at 17. Castor oil diya (lamp) were lit after sunset.

---

3 Modi, Narendra, 'Maa', *Narendra Modi.in*, https://tinyurl.com/bdh2xxpk. Accessed on 10 September 2025.

4 '*Gujarat Becomes First to Electrify All Villages*', *The Economic Times*, 13 November 2006, https://tinyurl.com/7e2vv3wa. Accessed on 10 September 2025.

Dark and dingy, without a waft of breeze during the long summers, eight heavily perspiring bodies were jammed together in the 480 square feet house, bitten by large mosquitoes which proliferated in the open drainage of the town. From June to September, the monsoons did bring some joy, even though it turned more humid and suffocating when it stopped raining. The only breather during the year was the winter when they huddled together under thin cotton blankets or jute cloth. To wake up before dawn was deliverance; a habit which has stayed with the Prime Minister.

There were no toothbrushes, toothpaste, showers, or even tap water in Modi's household. Teeth were brushed with crushed *neem* twigs. A clay pot of water was a luxury in summer when wells dried up. The reason perhaps why Narendra spent hours swimming in the Sharmishtha Lake, where he often washed laundry and bathed in public. A tailor paid a visit every two years or so to stitch clothes for members of the family from the same cheap cotton cloth. No newspaper was delivered at home. Murphy radio sets had made its appearance in Bombay, though not yet in Vadnagar homes. The first and only Aakashwani broadcasting station in Gujarat was set up by the Gaekwads of Baroda and had just begun operations in January 1947 with the playing of *Vande Mataram*.[5]

Dal, with gargantuan rotis of jowar and bajra having a pinch of salt, was roasted on a wood and cow dung-fed

5 Tere, Tushar, 'Sanskarnagari was first to hear 'akashvani' in Gujarat'. *The Times of India*, 13 February 2023, https://tinyurl.com/4j6wraut. Accessed on 10 September 2025.

fire, and consumed with green chilly paste, an antidote to appetite. Heeraba, recollects Modi, made delicious ghee from the cream, that his father brought. Wheat chapattis and veggies were prepared rarely. Tiny yellow-skinned bananas were a luxury, and apart from raw sour mangoes from the many Vadnagar orchards, Narendra must not have consumed more than two dozen Alphonso mangoes during his entire childhood, and that too, at community feasts. He loved to dunk the cold, hardened bajra roti in steaming hot tea.

Modi thus grew up in a household that was in that twilight zone between poor and lower middle class. Not starving yet barely surviving. He, as a child, watched his mother sitting on her haunches cleaning utensils of others. Modi imbibed first-hand the pains and stress of his mother, the Indian homemaker, whose life was a struggle without respite or hope.

Children like him learn early in life how not to embarrass their parents by demanding anything, not even the basic necessities. He was ultra-sensitive to the situation at home. He cooked *khichdi* for his siblings if his mother was ill, or was busy cleaning someone else's dirty utensils. He washed his family's clothes and bathed the home cow, the giver of sustenance. Making his parents feel that poverty was nothing to be embarrassed about. These childhood experiences shaped his later day approach towards the exhibitionist rich with blunted sensibilities.

Later, during his years as an RSS *pracharak*, Modi would come across grosser instances of abject poverty. A six-year-old child, watching sadly from a corner, saw the little milk kept for him being given away by his mother to an unexpected guest.

Many other such heart-wrenching episodes and spontaneous compassion for the poor led to his pragmatic solution-driven approach to address poverty at the grassroots.

Far away from the playing fields of Eton and Harrow and the hallowed portals of Oxbridge, primary school for Narendra was a eight room structure with blackboards written upon with squeaking chalk. The high school, which followed, was hardly different.

Rewind to sixty years before Narendra was born, just before the beginning of the 20th century, in stark contrast to Modi's childhood, Jawaharlal Nehru, India's first prime minister, was attended to, by English governesses and Irish tutors along with a retinue of liveried servants in a palatial 42-room home called Anand Bhawan of his barrister father, before studying at Harrow, where British aristocracy schooled their children, and Trinity College, Cambridge. Nehru writes in his autobiography that he had a garden, a tennis court and a swimming pool and a pet pony to ride. His childhood, he wrote, was sheltered and uneventful. His daughter, Indira, studied in posh schools in India and Switzerland, was fluent in French, and did a stint at Oxford.

Jawaharlal, the child, was aghast to watch his father sip imported red claret, which he thought was blood, as he puts it in his autobiography. Narendra, the child, watched his mother sitting on her haunches cleaning utensils of others with glass-mixed ash which often made her fingers bleed.

This comparison is relevant only to understand Modi's upbringing and early experiences which significantly impacted his mindset. His natural attunement with the poor and deeply ingrained grassroots socioeconomic philosophy, which is so different from his political opponents, is a result of this mindset.

As prime minister, due to political exigencies, Modi is compelled at times to attend events where there is an overt display of wealth. On such occasions, the revulsion he feels is evident from his hardened expression.

▪

Much has been written about his displaying leadership qualities at a young age (at ten, he led a procession to celebrate the formation of Gujarat State on May 1, 1960); his refusal to remain silent when injustice was perpetrated; his vigorous participation in debates, drama and other collective social activities. This would, of course, be true of most outstanding leaders. What is of interest however, is Narendra joining the Rashtriya Swayamsevak Sangh (RSS), despite his father's discomfiture, when he was eight; and a few years later, the thoughts which raced through his mind during and after the 1962 Sino-India and the 1965 India-Pakistan wars.

According to the *Shiva Purana* and *Skanda Purana*, at twelve places in India, the unmanifest Supreme, Lord Shiva, spontaneously appeared as a beam of infinite light, and each became a jyotirlinga. Near the Veraval coast in Southern Gujarat, in the historic town of Prabhas Patan, the first of the twelve jyotirlingas—the *aadi jyotirlinga*—is worshipped in one of the most ancient Shiva temples of India, Somnath, which is situated on the exact spot where the mythical Saraswati

River merges into the Arabian Sea. Somnath, an integral part of India's sacred geography, is the holiest of the holy. Repeatedly raided and desecrated by Islamic invaders, most notably, Muhammad Ghazni, who invaded India 17 times and, in 1025/26 CE, broke the sacred *jyotirlinga* at Somnath into pieces, after he had desecrated the *Baan Stambha* (arrow pillar) of the temple. After Ghazni, Alauddin Khilji and Aurangzeb too razed the Somnath temple.

Modi, as a teenager, was fascinated to read a popular trilogy of historical fiction by a Congress minister in Nehru's Cabinet and a prominent Gujarati author, Kanhaiyalal Munshi, titled *Patan ni Prabhuta, Gujarat no Nath* and *Rajadhiraj*; followed by the popular *Jai Somnath*, describing the absorbing political dynamics of the royals and the petty religious rivalries which had emboldened the Afghan invader, Ghazni, to repeatedly invade India, and wantonly destroy Somnath. Not only to plunder wealth, as whitewashed by the left leaning historians, but to further his idol-smashing religious iconoclasm

Modi learnt about the desecration of Somnath from his Hindi teacher, who ran the Vadnagar *shakha* of the RSS, or simply, the Sangh, as it is popularly known. The Sangh is today a 100-year-old powerhouse that has rendered stellar service to the Nation and enjoys enough goodwill and networking to make and sustain governments. Founded in 1925 by Dr Hedgewar, a Nagpur medico, inspired by the writings of Bal Gangadhar Tilak, Sri Aurobindo, and Vinayak Savarkar. Stripped of jargon, the objective of the RSS is to nourish Hindu culture; protect, unite, and galvanize Hindus, with the ultimate vision of ensuring the prosperity of the

Hindu Rashtra, a civilizational idea rather than a theocratic State. In 2024, it had a fiercely committed cadre of six million spread over its ubiquitous *shakhas* numbering more than 73,000. As the Sangh completes its centenary this year, Modi, in his address on 2025 Independence Day, called it the world's biggest NGO.

The story of Somnath brought tears to Narendra. He joined the *shakha* in Vadnagar, founded only six years before his birth, as a *bal swayamsevak*. RSS was then nowhere near the zenith of the influence it enjoys today. Post Gandhi's assassination, it had been banned by Nehru's government, which was revoked in 1949, a year before Narendra's birth.

There are no coincidences in life. Even though Narendra then obviously had no knowledge about RSS' purpose and intent, his karmic past was making the child gravitate towards an organization that would shape his future. The iron discipline and a single line of command in the Sangh endeared itself to Narendra who learnt to execute errands and the tasks given to him unquestioningly.

Narendra was twelve when the Indo-China war, or border skirmish, as some have termed it, broke out in October 1962. Modi has always bore great love for the men in uniform; whether soldiers or *swayamsevaks* of the Sangh. In 1962, he took great pride in serving free glasses of hot tea to the soldiers, travelling by train on their way to the frontier. He spent many nights, during the war, sleeping on the Mehsana railway platform, from where trains proceeded to Delhi. Years later, he was enraged at reading accounts of how the Indian government, complacent in believing that China was a friend, and in a state of total military unpreparedness, had lost the war. V.K. Krishna Menon, the then defence minister, a man with palpable communist leanings, had influenced his friend, Nehru, into believing that Mao's China would never invade India. China overran Indian military posts in Aksai Chin, an area of 37,000 sq. kms in the Western Himalayas, and still controls it. Nehru had earlier in 1959 while speaking in the Rajya Sabha dismissed the significance of Aksai Chin as a strategic territory describing it as 'barren, uninhabited region without a vestige of grass and 17,000 ft. high.'[6]

During this war, school children all over India, including Narendra were taught to sing patriotic songs, including one in Gujarati, ironically titled *taiyaar thai jajo* (Be Prepared). The teenage Narendra instinctively knew that India had been on the back foot and had narrowly managed to salvage its position. Decades later, Modi learnt that the situation in 1962 was so desperate (the Chinese troops had reached Assam) that it had compelled ministers to visit a powerful Durga temple of Pitambara Devi at Datia near Gwalior to participate in a yagna, after which the Chinese had suddenly and inexplicably declared a unilateral ceasefire and withdrawn to the prewar position, except for Aksai Chin.

Three years later, in 1965, Narendra saw the fiercest of all India-Pakistan wars, when Ayub Khan decided to test the mettle of the new Prime Minister Lal Bahadur Shastri. After infiltration attempts in Kashmir failed, the Pakistan Army

---

6 Rajya Sabha. *Short Notice Question, 31 August 1959. Rajya Sabha Debates*, p. 2283. Rajya Sabha Secretariat, 1959, PDF File, https://tinyurl.com/3xhuvw6a. Accessed on 10 September 2025.

brazenly invaded Kashmir by crossing the Line-of-Control (LoC). In the most intense tank warfare since World War II, both countries lost roughly 300 tanks and 5,000 men each. The war was pronounced to be a partial victory for India, resulting in Ayub Khan and Shastri signing a ceasefire pact at Tashkent. Within hours of the signing, Shastri suddenly died, ostensibly of a heart attack, in a shroud of yet unresolved mystery.

This time, the war had been much closer home (it started with skirmishes in the Rann of Kutch, 253 kilometres from Vadnagar) with blackouts every night (Narendra was one of the blackouts 'enforcers' in Vadnagar). Air raid sirens screamed often. Narendra listened to war bulletins on All-India Radio, at a well-to-do friend's house. The same serving–tea–and–snacks–to–soldiers routine on the trains followed. The teenager was saddened by Shastri's death and incensed at the generals of Pakistan. More than 5000 Indian servicemen had been martyred. Slightly better prepared than 1962, the still under-equipped Indian Army witnessed officers throwing themselves under Pakistani Patton tanks in an act of supreme sacrifice.

Modi now seriously considered joining the Indian Army. His young blood was bristling with rage. He vividly remembers a soldier in the 4th Battalion, the Grenadiers of the Indian Army, called Abdul Hamid, a poor tailor's son, who, in the Khem Karan sector, destroyed eight Pakistani tanks single handedly and was martyred while destroying the ninth. Hamid was posthumously awarded India's highest military honour, the Param Vir Chakra. Decades later, on

9th October 2013, Hamid's widow, Rasoolan Bibi, a resident of Ghazipur of Uttar Pradesh, though old and ailing, along with her two children, came to meet Modi, who presented her with a shawl. A tearful Bibi blessed Modi to serve the nation for long.

■

Indira Gandhi became India's prime minister. Had someone then predicted that a poor boy from Vadnagar would humble the Nehru-Gandhis and wrest power from them, none would have believed.

A child's intelligence and mental makeup are influenced by both genetic and environmental factors. The most robust child development comes from supportive environments that allow the genetic potential to flourish. Narendra Modi turned this conventional wisdom about genetics and environment upside down.

Narendra received the most basic, near substandard, education in the Gujarati medium up to his matriculation. Neither his parents nor his elder brothers were in any position to impart knowledge or information to him. He did not have access to daily newspapers or the radio. The Vadnagar *shakha* of the Sangh was a source of limited information. Modi's meteoric rise is therefore not attributable to any genetic or environmental advantage. Damodardas Modi's underprivileged household producing an international leader of Modi's calibre has to be attributed to Modi's own past karma, the dint of his breathtaking commitment and zeal, and the protection he has constantly received from the Divine Mother or *Jagat Janani* as he addresses Her. How meticulously destiny was preparing Modi for his mission is evident from his childhood, which prematurely ended with his matriculation at 17. The child learnt the value of every morsel of food prepared by his frail mother, who had undergone labour pain six times without any nutrition or pregnancy care. Wood and cow dung fed stoves meant watery eyes throughout the day. Modi's government has created so far more than 11 crore smoke-free kitchens by providing free LPG connections.

Washing laundry in a public place and drawing water from the well, which had no pulley or pump. Relentlessly, without a single pause for 365 days. No cooking gas; no tap water; no ceiling fan; no holidays and no vacations. Further aggravated by moonlighting in other households. His mother was not the only Superwoman, Narendra witnessed. He saw millions of them across the country. He resolved as a teenager to alleviate their suffering. This explains the immense joy that Modi feels today when schoolgirls have separate toilets and free cooking gas cylinders are distributed to women all over the country.

Did ancient Vadnagar, bristling with centuries of spirituality, karma-connect with Modi or did the soul occupying Modi's mind and body choose Vadnagar as the optimal setting for fulfilling the purpose of his incarnation or was it orchestrated by the forces, mentioned by Tagore and Sri Aurobindo, who occasionally course-correct India's destiny? Be as it may, there is not an iota of doubt that Narendra Modi's first seventeen years in Vadnagar shaped his core value system, his socioeconomic philosophy, and his lifelong dedication to the Sangh. Like an expert sculptor, Narendra's mental and emotional makeup was chiselled in childhood by the makers of the blueprint of India's destiny.

Those nameless millions who toil day after day without begging or complaining about economic hardship. The iron discipline of the Sangh which performed each task so efficiently. The emotional bond with the soldiers forged during the Sino-India and the India-Pakistan wars. The toilers, the soldiers, and the Sangh—Modi's childhood sweethearts—would remain his lifelong love.

Destiny was meticulously preparing Narendra Modi to take on the Dynasty.

CHAPTER TWO

Cutting Ties

NARENDRA'S SPIRITUALITY WAS seeded in early childhood. Apart from recurring early morning dreams of Ganesha, the elephant-headed God of auspicious beginnings, regarded as a cosmic sign of all-around spiritual protection, Narendra was fascinated by the many ancient temples in his hometown, particularly the Giripuri Mahadev. Like Somnath on the Veraval coast, this temple housed an ancient linga to which Narendra often made the traditional offering of a spoonful of milk and leaves of the wood apple tree called bilipatra, symbolic of surrendering one's ego to the formless Lord Shiva.

Modi has written in a blog that since childhood, his mother felt that his mindset was different from his siblings.[7] The romantic daydreaming of a teenager never touched Narendra. On the contrary, he had a firm belief that he was not destined to undergo the normal life cycle of marriage,

---

7 Modi, Narendra, 'Maa'. *Narendra Modi.in*, https://tinyurl.com/bdh2xxpk. Accessed on 10 September 2025.

parenthood and retirement. The meaninglessness of normality became increasingly evident to the teenaged Narendra. One constant feeling never left him that his life mission was inextricably connected with the Sangh, and through the Sangh, his country. When Narendra was a year old, the Bhartiya Jan Sangh, predecessor of the Bharatiya Janata Party, was founded by Dr Syama Prasad Mookerjee, earlier a member of Nehru's Cabinet.

Apart from playing *Kho Kho*, or cricket with a rubber ball and makeshift stumps, or swimming in the Sharmista Lake, there was nothing in Vadnagar to entertain or distract young Narendra. Except, of course, his strong attraction to worship at the many temples of Vadnagar. A spiritual journey often begins with an intense desire to worship and spend time in temples. And Vadnagar bristled with temples.

Apart from the Giripuri Mahadev temple mentioned earlier, Narendra emulated his mother, who constantly chanted *Sitaram*, and began intoning the *Mahamrityunjaya mantra* at the 17th century Hatkeshwar temple's inner sanctum sanctorum housing a *swayambhu shivalinga*. He also frequented the Durga temple in Ambawadi; and enjoyed roaming in the ruins of Buddhist monasteries. He took excursions to the gorgeous *Surya* (Sun) Temple at Modhera, in Mehsana district. To control his palate, the most difficult of all the senses to conquer, he at times gave up eating salt, chilly, oil and jaggery, or sometimes not eating food grains and having only milk. However, the most significant event in Modi's spiritual journey occurred when he read a Gujarati biography of his namesake, Narendra Viswanath Dutta, known to the world as Swami Vivekananda.

In the Indian spiritual firmament, none shines more brightly than Sri Ramakrishna, described by Romain Rolland as, '[T]he consummation of two thousand years of the spiritual life of three hundred million people.'[8] An illiterate priest of the Kali temple at Dakshineswar, a few kilometres north of Kolkata, Ramakrishna was in a constant divine-intoxicated state, who beheld the Divine Mother, his Kali, in every nook and corner. Vivekananda became the prime disciple of Ramakrishna.

Vivekananda's life story made a huge impact upon Narendra who read and re-read the Gujarati biography. At this stage, Narendra was impressed by how Vivekananda had mesmerized the world within his short life span of 39 years. Instances of Vivekananda's deep power of thought, keen intelligence and extraordinary memory impressed him. Vivekananda, being overnight reduced to a state of poverty following the death of his lawyer father and his subsequent struggle for survival, struck a chord in Narendra's heart.

Vivekananda's lecture at the World's Parliament of Religions at Chicago in 1893, explaining the essence of the Gita, taught Narendra that each human was an imperishable soul, provided with the temporary vehicles of body and mind, to work out each incarnation. The body and mind would perish at death, with only the soul returning to the Father's house, to await reincarnation. Like his hero, Narendra began to consider renouncing society and becoming a monk.

---

8 Rolland, Romain, 'To My Western Readers', *The Life of Ramakrishna*, Advaita Ashram, Almora, 1931, p. 14

His decision to finally leave home at 17 was thus greatly influenced by Vivekananda. It was only much later that Modi would grasp the extent of the extremely exalted spiritual status of Vivekananda, probably beyond even his guru, Sri Ramakrishna.

At this early age, Narendra lost all fear of death. He often thought of the martyred soldiers in the two wars with China and Pakistan, and his desire to avenge their sacrifices grew intense. Spirituality taught him that to sacrifice the body for the country was an honour and a privilege.

A restlessness began to pervade Narendra as he turned sixteen. Within months, he would be promoted to the 11th standard, followed by an examination conducted by the Gujarat Secondary School Certificate Examination Board, or SSC, as it was popularly known. This exam was based on a curriculum that had remained unaltered for half a century and involved rote learning, which Narendra was least inclined to do. He was exasperated with the constant refrain of his teachers that, although he possessed an excellent memory and outstanding articulation skills, why did his academic performance lag.

Interacting with the soldiers on the train during the two wars had fascinated him. He loved his time with the National Cadet Corps (NCC). As Prime Minister, Modi has never missed a single opportunity to hail the NCC for inspiring Indian youth for nation building and instilling discipline. The NCC has played a crucial role in disaster management, the *Swachh Bharat* Movement, and the *Beti Bachao, Beti Padhao* initiative of the Modi government. From 14 lakhs cadets in

2014, the number has increased to 20 lakhs including 8 lakhs girl cadets.[9] Modi has extolled NCC cadets for excelling in sports at national and international levels. NCC, as old as independent India, is today the world's largest uniformed youth organization.

Clear the SSC exams, and join the Indian Army became a recurring thought. He was conscious that this path would meet with resistance from his family. His father often admonished him for spending far too much time in the Sangh instead of concentrating on studies. Damodardas resolutely refused Narendra's request to join a nearby Sainik school on one ground or the other.

Narendra had heard vague rumours that he had been betrothed when he was a child to a girl in a neighbouring village, in accordance with the custom of his caste. Marriage arranged or otherwise, he felt, did not align with his objective to dedicate his entire life to serving people.

*Pracharak*s of the Sangh were his heroes. A *pracharak* is no ordinary member; for all practical purposes, he is a monk without the orange robe. A *pracharak* had to dedicate his entire life to the RSS, and therefore only the unmarried could become *Pracharak*s, with only a few exceptions for agrarian areas where marriage is an economic necessity.

Between 3.30 and 4.00 a.m. every morning, Narendra's eyes began to open involuntarily. He had learnt in the Sangh

---

9 'English rendering of PM's speech at NCC Rally at the Cariappa Parade Ground in Delhi'. *Press Information Bureau, Government of India*, 27 January 2025, https://tinyurl.com/3m6sfe84. Accessed on 10 September 2025.

that only the spiritually evolved woke up during this period, termed as the *brahmamoorat*, when the probability of an individual soul communicating with the Cosmic Consciousness was the greatest. He sprang up from bed, sat cross-legged and intoned the all-powerful *Gayatri Mantra* (translated by Swami Vivekananda as 'we meditate on the glory of that Being who has produced the Universe; may She enlighten our minds'). This mantra purified his intellect. Sever all family ties which prevented him from full time service to the Sangh and the country. This became Narendra's all-encompassing thought.

After appearing for his SSC exams in March 1967, Narendra decided that the time to exit home was now. Not surreptitiously, but after informing all concerned. One late afternoon, seizing an opportune moment, Narendra informed his mother, the person dearest to him, about his resolve to quit. Heeraba was hardly surprised but saddened. A visiting *sadhu*, after reviewing Narendra's horoscope, had told her that Narendra, then 13, would become either a saint or a ruler. Many years later, Modi's friends had burst into laughter when an astrologer from Bihar had made an identical prediction. Heeraba instinctively knew that this child of hers, was, for a better word, different. Like any mother, she was concerned as what this unusual child would do. Narendra's nonconformist style was evident to his family. Not attending a family wedding of his youngest aunt to tend to a *sadhu* visiting the Giripuri Mahadev temple, was one such instance.

After considerable discussion, an unsatisfactory solution was imposed upon Narendra to take admission in a science college in neighbouring Visnagar. Narendra did not though really attend this college. Years later, following the counsel of his lifelong mentor in the Sangh—Laxman Rao Inamdar or Vakil Saheb—Modi obtained degrees in political science from Delhi University and Gujarat University, both by correspondence.

In mid-May 1968, Narendra had to undergo an unregistered marriage ceremony according to Vedic rites. While the girl was 16, Narendra was not yet 18. Within days of the ceremony, on 3rd June 1968, Narendra left home permanently.

Like all Indian schoolboys, Narendra had learnt about the two princes of ancient India, possibly contemporaries, who had overnight walked out of their palaces, leaving behind their beautiful wives and children, to search for a solution for the suffering humanity, and later founded two world religions: Buddhism and Jainism.

No able-bodied and intelligent teenager so resolutely determines to move away from the normal pattern of life. And certainly not one having an electrifying popular personality, full of life, like Narendra. All his five siblings lived normal and ordinary family-centred lives. His father was highly displeased with Narendra's decision, though he ultimately accepted it.

Compassion generates in many a heart. However, it is rare that a person translates this compassion into active lifelong service of all people. Narendra had not an iota of doubt that his life was designed to be exclusively dedicated to service, which was inimical to family life. When he became the Gujarat Chief Minister, and someone claiming to be his relative, asked a government secretary for a favour, Modi bluntly and categorically told his Secretaries and staff that '*Modi no koi sago nathi!*' (Modi has no relatives).

He clinically severed all family ties save and except with his mother and has never felt a twinge of regret in doing so. Stoic, detached, and resolute, Narendra Modi was ready to follow the dictates of Bharata Bhagya Vidhata.

CHAPTER THREE

Sadhana & Siddhi

NARENDRA MODI, NOT yet an adult, with the barest of belongings in a cloth sling bag and less than two hundred rupees earned by lugging edible oil containers for a merchant in Vadnagar, armed by the protective red vermilion tilak placed by his mother between his eyebrows to cover the proverbial third eye, feeling liberated and excited, sat in a slow moving passenger train from Mehsana to Old Delhi station in a crammed unreserved third class compartment. His umbilical cord was cut a second time.

His long journey over two years would take him over the snow-clad Himalayas up to 19,000 feet without oxygen or warm clothes, to the Ramakrishna Mission's maths and colleges in Bengal, to the forests surrounding Guwahati in Assam, to Almora in what is now Uttarakhand, to desert hamlets in Rajasthan, to literally hundreds of temples, including the famed Shakti peeths. He would walk for miles, often sitting in trains without a ticket, hitching a lift on trucks carrying goods, sleeping in temples and sanatoria for pilgrims, even on stone platforms in crematoria, eating at langars or free temple kitchens or a hospitable stranger's home. Diving in ice-cold rivers and nearly getting killed by lightning under a tree. Loving all the time, the aroma of his motherland's soil.

This was not the restless roaming in the dark by a boy on the threshold of manhood. Narendra constantly felt that someone was watching over him. Someone who whispered over his right shoulder. Some would have said that it was his solar angel or guardian spirit. He felt energy being transmitted to him from unknown sources. When sitting cross-legged before a deity in a temple, he began to spontaneously meditate. At times, he felt Bhairava was protecting him. He had a feeling of déjà vu in the ruins of forts and ancient towns. Fearless, relishing the solitude at night, and chatting during the day with strangers.

He began travelling with groups of sadhus of different sects and callings. Cooking food for them and carrying their belongings, hoping to receive some grace or spiritual insight. One afternoon walking through the Garbhanga forest, thirty-one kilometres from Guwahati, he spotted a small, highly emaciated mendicant with remarkably sparkling eyes, in a grass hut. He gestured to Narendra to sit down. His face was splendidly radiant at close quarters.

For the next thirty days, the man relentlessly stared at Narendra without uttering a word. He appeared to be transmitting energy to Narendra. The man neither ate nor slept. Instinctively, Narendra did not ask him any questions. His hut and the little garden around it appeared to be ring-fenced from the wild animals lurking in the forest. He conjured up for his guest an unchanging meal of boiled rice and dal every afternoon, though Narendra never saw him cooking. The sage advised him that he should forget the idea of becoming a monk or a renunciate. He hinted that Narendra's destiny had a different path. That of service to the people.

Narendra's journey then took him to the Kamakhya temple in Guwahati. Legend has it that Parvati or Shakti, Shiva's consort, incensed by her father insulting Shiva in public, took her own life, which made Shiva furious, and he did a *tandava* or a dance of destruction during which he flung the body of Parvati into fifty-one different body parts, which fell on earth, and each of them became a *Shaktipeeth*. The first and foremost of these Shaktipeeths, where the female genitalia fell, is the ancient Kamakhya temple in Guwahati, built by the God of Love, Kamadev, himself, according to lore. Appropriately called the temple of desire.

When Narendra descended the pitch-dark staircase to reach the inner sanctum of the temple and dipped his hand in the flowing water, he experienced a tremendous burst of energy in his chest as if it would explode. He enjoyed meditating in the temple complex and walked around the periphery of the temple 108 times.

He learnt about the ten Mahavidhyas, all manifestations of Shakti, from the Sadhus. His love for, and unflinching faith in, the Divine Mother, his Jagat Janani, grew intense. Years later, when he was a *pracharak*, every night before retiring to bed, he shared his innermost thoughts with Her, recorded in a small notebook in Gujarati, he carried with him. He noted his inner feelings of fear, sorrow, and conflict; and felt that he was constantly shielded by a bigger force. He inexplicably self-destructed most of these jottings, and barely a few survive. Those surviving jottings in Gujarati were translated into English and published a few years ago.

Universal compassion and service to all is a recurring theme in these jottings, which are in the form of a dialogue with Her. Modi is conscious, even in December 1986, that every moment of his life is precious. Interestingly, he prays to the Divine Mother to empower him to assess people 'beyond masks and beyond words', and to decipher the right from the wrong.

'I want to light a lamp in every feeble, dreamless eye,' aspires Narendra. He was aware that he had been blessed with a sharp intuition. He reverentially records the words of Vivekananda, who said that the fulfilment of desires of the downtrodden is the only truth and real power. Narendra constantly dreamt of a prosperous India. He vaguely sensed that he was being prepared by destiny for a role on a larger platform.

Narendra's sojourns took him to Almora, situated at the foothills of the Kumaon Himalayas, to visit the Vivekananda centre located there. He was magically drawn to the village of Kasar Devi, a few kilometres away and visited the second-century Temple of Kasar Devi dedicated to Durga, as well as to Shiva and Bhairav. Modi had read in Vivekananda's diary that the sage had spent a considerable time meditating in a cave in the temple complex, commanding breathtaking views of the Nanda Devi, Trishul and Panchauli ranges. Modi meditated near the same cave on the Kartik Poornima day and found himself overwhelmed with tears of joy.

Kasar Devi is one of the three spots in the world where geomagnetic activity is at its highest (Machu Picchu in Peru and Stonehenge in England being the other two). These places exhibit a strong 'Van Allen radiation belt effect' due to their intense and unusual magnetic fields. This temple bursts with profound serenity and palpable energy. Apart from Vivekananda, over the years, this temple has had many famous visitors, including George Harrison of the Beatles, the famed Indian mystic, Anandmayi Ma, the singer, Bob Dylan, and the Danish seer, Alfred Sorensen.

Modi's unflinching faith in the Divine Mother grew exponentially during these two years of discovering his spiritual self. His maturity and thinking far transcended any teenager, as the seeds of spirituality sowed in his childhood were sprouting in his youth. He felt an inner call to worship at temples dedicated to different Mahavidhyas.

From Uttar Pradesh, he crossed over to the border of Madhya Pradesh in Datia where he was spellbound by a temple dedicated to Bagalamukhi, the extremely powerful goddess having the visage of a heron or crane. He also prayed at another Bagalamukhi temple at Nalkheda, near Ujjain. If your cause was just, she destroyed your enemy. One has to be careful not to take Her name in vain. It was at the Datia temple that the yagna was performed during the 1962 Indian Chinese War. Next to Her, in the Datia temple complex, Narendra had the rare darshan of Kali in the form of a widow,

Dhumavati, whose worship is forbidden for married women. He worshipped an ancient *shivalinga* in the courtyard of the temple.

He witnessed the *ugra swaroop* of one of the Mahavidhyas as Kali, both at Kalighat in Kolkata, another shaktipeeth, where the toe of the right foot of the Goddess fell during the Shiva *tandava*, and at nearby Dakshineswar on the bank of the Hooghly River, the temple where Ramakrishna had met Vivekananda.

At the Manikarnika ghat at Varanasi, Narendra once came across sadhus from the Shaiva sect who were possibly Aghoris.

Aghora is the advanced discipline of Tantra, the left-hand path to God. Aghora, in Sanskrit, means, that which is beyond fear. Aghoris worship Lord Shiva in the fierce form of Bhairava as the Supreme Reality. Also, Shakti in the form of Smashan Tara. The practitioners of Aghora transcend all dualities, are classic stoics, and make no distinction between good and evil; pure and impure, austerity and luxury. The divine love of Smashan Tara is not for the weak-hearted. To experiment without a guru may prove fatal.

The sincere and rigorous *sadhana* on the *aghori* path leads to acquiring siddhis which go far beyond all laws of physics known to mankind. These extraordinary abilities include control over all beings.

Narendra often lost track of time during his journeys. Only when he reached a railway station that he knew the exact day and month. Sporadically, he thought of posting a message in Gujarati on a five-paise postcard to his mother just to allay her apprehensions about his well-being but did not. Slightly more than two years had passed, and he now sported an unkempt beard and long hair. Although in the pink of health, some of the spiritual practices that he had learnt were bringing about changes in his cell consciousness and exhausting him a bit mentally and emotionally. He had little doubt that he had reconnected with his yogic past. Despite the advice of the sage in Guwahati, some remnants of his desire to become a monk with the Ramakrishna Mission survived. He decided to have a last go at the Rajkot Ramakrishna mission.

Narendra got goose pimples when Swami Atmasthananda, in charge of the Rajkot mission, repeated almost the exact words of the sage that he should forget about being a monk and that his destiny lay elsewhere. Strangely, he was not at all disappointed. His mind was made up and he knew what he had to do.

Vadnagar was not too far from Rajkot, and he decided to return home and dedicate his entire life to the Sangh. Someone then suggested him to visit Dwarahat. He remembered vaguely reading about this place. He backtracked and reached Ranikhet, fifteen kilometres away was Dwarahat, known as the Village of Temples, some of them dating back to the 10th century.

Three kilometres from Dwarahat, in the serene village of Kukuchina, was the cave, where the ageless, deathless saint of India, Mahavatar Babaji, had initiated Lahiri Mahasaya in Kriya Yoga in 1861. In 1970, the uphill climb to the cave was extremely difficult. Modi has been a lifelong exponent of Kriya Yoga, which energizes him at dawn. One wonders whether Mahavatar Babaji gave a Darshan at any time to Narendra Modi. Many believe that Babaji is the custodian of ancient Hindu culture and spiritual knowledge.

It is interesting to read what Paramhansa Yogananda has said about Babaji in his *Autobiography of a Yogi.* He described Babaji as the deathless master who had preserved the same youthful form for centuries, perhaps even millennia. Babaji seldom appeared in public, choosing instead to guide humanity through his chosen disciples. Transcending the ordinary laws of physics, he could appear and disappear at will. His spiritual state was beyond human comprehension, for the limited vision of men could not reach this transcendent star.[10] Many other saints and seers of different sects, over the years, have recorded their meeting Mahavatar Babaji.

No genuine spiritual seeker discloses the intricacies of his sadhana, or his Master(s) or Guru(s) or how he was initiated. Nor does he flippantly brag about his siddhis. In many ways, this period of more than two years was perhaps the most crucial in preparing Narendra Modi for his ultimate mission. Even an atheist or agnostic will not fail to notice the many extraordinary abilities of Modi, including his limitless reserves of energy, faultless intuition and spellbinding charisma, which transcend the mere human.

When he returned to Vadnagar after more than two years, Narendra stayed for barely 24 hours so as not to raise the hopes of his family that he would settle down. He had roamed

---

10 Yogananda, Paramhansa, 'Chapter 33: Babaji, the Yogi-Christ of Modern India', *Autobiography of a Yogi,* Jaico, Mumbai, 1958, pp. 297-298

the country for more than two years. Upon his return, he achieved his burning ambition to become a *swayamsevak* of the Sangh. His overjoyed mother found a tattered woolen shawl, books on Vivekananda, a change of clothes, and her photograph in the cloth sling bag of her son.

CHAPTER FOUR

Gujarat No Nath & Agnipariksha

MODI'S FAVOURITE AUTHOR, Kanhaiyalal Munshi, weaved a most intricate plot in the second book of his historical fiction trilogy titled Gujarat no Nath, meaning the Lord and Protector of Gujarat.

Siddharaj Jaisinh of the Solanki dynasty in the 12th century, a wise, brave and culturally polished ruler of Gujarat, endeavours to unite and rule justly. He faces a plethora of problems from his intellectual but naïve prime minister, Munjal; his cunning opponent, Uda Mehta; his formidable mother, Meenal Devi, who loves Munjal; and Kak, a clever, pragmatic warrior who becomes his go-to man. The King faces internal rebellion and external threats as also political conspiracy, including betrayal in court, resistance from the nobles and manipulation from religious leaders. Finally, he is victorious and emerges as Gujarat no Nath.

Munshi could have well been writing about Gujarat,

a hotbed of intrigue and unprincipled mercenaries who masqueraded as political leaders, on all sides of the political spectrum, when Modi, as a Sangh worker, entered the scene sometime in early 1972.

Both as a *swayamsevak* and later as a *pracharak*, Narendra Modi endeared himself to all in the Sangh with his 24/7, 365-days commitment, from sweeping the floor, washing clothes to serving breakfast and tea, to efficiently organizing national camps. He spoke little but when he did, the seniors listened to this rising star. And then came Indira's infamous Emergency.

When Indira Gandhi declared Emergency on 26 June 1975, Narendra, a young *pracharak* of 24 years, immersed himself in the struggle of resistance against the Emergency in Gujarat. In the darkest hour of India's democracy, with virtually every leader of the opposition in jail without trial, the press censored, the judiciary muzzled, and civil liberties suspended, came the moment of reckoning for Narendra.

In a span of just four years, Modi's discipline and reliability, combined with his daredevil nature, were already known to many in the Sangh. Narendra was therefore inundated with several sensitive assignments like translating anti-Emergency literature into Gujarati and distributing it across the state and other parts of India, delivering messages to senior leaders of the Sangh in jail, and looking after the families of those imprisoned as also organizing secret meetings. Avoid arrest at all costs, Modi was instructed. He need not have been.

Like the Scarlet Pimpernel, Modi managed to remain out of the grasp of the police. A consummate escape artist walking in and out of police stations, jails and other government offices, disguised sometimes as a Sikh or a saffron-clad Swamiji. Single-handedly, he secreted away those leaders who had still not been arrested to safe houses organized by him. Keeping visiting leaders like the firebrand George Fernandes safe, and spreading the message of resistance amongst fearful people, Narendra managed to evade arrest repeatedly in a near miraculous fashion. He used to look directly into the eyes of a suspicious policeman and exercise mental control through his penetrating gaze. Managing to outwit them with his razor-sharp intelligence, his ability to talk himself out of any tricky situation, and his uncanny instincts. Working 24/7 was usual for him. Although Modi was hyperactive and took maximum risks, he was not arrested, unlike some of his other co-workers. Like Sri Aurobindo, who, during his revolutionary days, used his spiritual siddhis to bamboozle the British police.

Nanaji Deshmukh, a most revered leader of the Sangh, was on the list of every police station in the country. The then 59-year-old Nanaji had somehow managed to evade arrest. The Gujarat police had spread its dragnet far and wide to arrest him. Narendra contacted Natubhai, a Gujarati theatre personality, and asked for his senior make-up man to help him. They got hold of a barber to clean shave Nanaji's head, made a few changes on his face, and fitted him with Gandhi-style glasses, Deshmukh became instantly unrecognizable. Decades later, Deshmukh, for his outstanding services to India, would posthumously be awarded the Bharat Ratna. *Sangharsh ma Gujarat*, Modi's memoirs during the Emergency, became popular.

Due to the Emergency, Modi's near religious reverence and inner respect for preserving the Constitution at all costs, strengthened. 26 June 1975, the black day in India's history when the Emergency was declared, would later be termed by Modi and the BJP, as the *Samvidhan Hatya Diwas* (the day on which the Constitution was murdered).

Modi says that he likes to constantly feel the pulse of the people and verify his thought processes by consulting a cross section of political forces in the state. He interacted freely with workers belonging to other political parties like the Jamat-e-Islami-Hind, the Gandhians, members of the Morarji Desai faction of the Congress, the Communists and Socialists.

In the early and mid-1980s, Modi loved interacting with those he called the 90 Not Out Club of highly revered nonagenarian Gandhians like Prabhudas Patwari, Shankarlal Banker, Ravishankar Maharaj and Acharya Kripalani, from whom he imbibed a deep understanding of the Gandhian philosophy of service as also the Mahatma's mindset.

Modi's extensive underground work during the Emergency naturally did not go unnoticed by the Sangh's national leaders, who, sensing Modi's great political acumen, decided, in 1985, to 'loan' him to the BJP, where his rise would be more dramatic.

In January 1987, Modi was appointed as the organizing secretary (Gujarat) of the BJP. In a heavily Congress-dominated political landscape, he carved a win for the BJP in the Ahmedabad municipal elections (though a gang lord, Abdul Latif, defiantly won in five out of eight wards). In 1990, he excelled in managing the Gujarat leg of Advani's

Rath Yatra, starting from the sacrosanct Somnath temple, standing proud after multiple desecrations over centuries. Planned to culminate in Ayodhya, where stood the Babri Masjid, the emerging Bihar leader, Lalu Prasad Yadav, scuttled the *yatra* in Patna.

Then came the meteoric jump for Modi. He was appointed as one of the seventeen members of the BJP's National Election Committee for the 1991 elections, which the Congress won on the sympathy wave following Rajiv Gandhi's assassination by Tamil separatists in Sri Lanka. In December 1991, Modi became prominent after managing the Ekta Yatra of the BJP from Kanyakumari to Kashmir, where he, along with Murli Manohar Joshi, dramatically unfurled the National Flag, after declining security protection against a possible terrorist attack by Kashmiri separatists who were at their peak. Modi's organizational credentials and his eye for the minutest detail became a talking point in political circles.

Modi was now in the limelight. Many in the party were envious of the 41-year-old Modi's rise and rise. But none more than one man—Shankersinh Vaghela.

Vaghela, addressed as *bapu* by his followers, perpetually had this contemptuous smile on his face, which made anyone meeting him distinctly nervous. Tall, heavy built with bulging eyes, Vaghela's impressive oratory was clever, carping and sarcastic. He had joined Jana Sangh and then the BJP and rose to be its President in Gujarat. Vaghela desperately wanted to be the chief minister. Keshubhai Patel was Vaghela's main rival, whom Modi supported. Though that was not the only reason why Vaghela disliked Modi. Bapu had a great nose for sensing trouble. He had correctly guessed that one day Narendra Modi would be a far greater rival. He summarily jettisoned Modi from his team.

Narendra Modi simply shrugged his shoulders and walked away to work for the party in the assembly elections due in five states, as well as to work on his pet project of a school called Sanskardham in Ahmedabad, which he had started in the memory of his Sangh mentor, Vakil Saheb.

Fast forward to early 1995, when the stage was set for the BJP to gain power in Gujarat, with Vaghela confident of becoming the chief minister. Modi's organizational abilities were appreciated by the BJP, as it secured 121 out of 182 seats. However, at the last minute, it was Keshubhai who was appointed as the chief minister, in a political plot, which would have made Kanhaiya Lal Munshi look like a novice. Bapu was mad with rage at Modi. If Modi was not in the picture, Bapu would have outwitted Keshubhai.

There are no adjectives adequate to describe Vaghela's political career. His single-minded, unwavering commitment to the cause was evident to all, and that cause was called Shankersinh Vaghela. Nothing happened in Gujarat that Narendra did not know. Modi knew that the fuming and highly impatient Vaghela would soon rebel and was in back-door touch with the Congress. Vaghela did rebel, and as a compromise, Keshubhai, after just seven and a half months in power, was replaced with Suresh Mehta, a Vaghela nominee. Bapu imposed one more condition, namely, banish Modi from Gujarat. With pleasure, said Narendra Modi and walked out. Vaghela was both nervous and puzzled. Vaghela did not know what a huge favour he had unwittingly done to Modi.

In November 1995, Advani promptly appointed Modi as the National Secretary of the BJP, requiring him to be based in New Delhi. During those years of exile from Gujarat, Narendra Modi organized the party and strengthened his contacts at all levels. He enjoyed being once again in the Himalayas, and visited many foreign countries for the party. He used the time to learn computers and technology. Significantly, Narendra also renewed some of the spiritual connects of his youthful initiation, as he found time to further his sadhana.

In the meanwhile, the Vaghela–Keshubhai–Mehta slugfest merrily continued. Bapu lost his Lok Sabha seat, left the BJP, and formed his own party, which was supported by the Congress, making Vaghela achieve his lifelong ambition to be the chief minister of Gujarat but only for a year, when he was forced to resign. He wound up his party and joined the Congress. Unfortunately for Bapu, the March 1998 assembly elections were handsomely won by the BJP, and the old warhorse Keshubhai became the chief minister again. In May 1998, Modi was promoted as General Secretary at a national level.

In two years, Vaghela had changed three political parties. Later, Vaghela would change three more, the Jan Vikalpa Morcha, the NCP of Sharad Pawar, the Praja Shakti Democratic Party, all with dismal results. Finally, he again campaigned for the Congress in 2022. His frequent party changing was so confusing that at a Jain religious function where Vaghela was the chief guest, and which this writer attended, the organizers repeatedly corrected themselves as to which political party Vaghela belonged to. He appeared quite nonchalant and amused.

While the real Gujarat no Nath bided his time in New Delhi, Keshubhai bumbled and bungled through several natural disasters like cyclone, floods and the Bhuj earthquake which befell the state, and was proving to be an embarrassment for the BJP whose political graph was in decline, and defeat in the forthcoming 2003 Gujarat assembly elections was a distinct possibility.

Both Vajpayee and Advani realized that the Gujarat BJP badly required the magic wand of Narendra Modi, who had received a five-minute standing ovation from a 50,000-strong audience at a function in Ahmedabad to commemorate the struggle against Indira's Emergency, for his role in the resistance. They directed a slightly trifle Narendra Modi to overnight takeover of the post of Chief Minister of Gujarat. The first time that Modi would occupy a public office.

Narendra Modi has felt throughout that he is a child of destiny, propelled according to a preordained plan to execute his mission. Senior leaders with a gigantic reputation had tried to cut him short, to banish him from political life and placed seemingly insurmountable obstacles in his career. Knives were out for him all the time. At every critical turn in life, Modi sensed that a powerful force was protecting him, guiding him, directing him. Somebody said that he has *Shatrunjay Yog* in his horoscope. No enemy would be able to vanquish him.

Narendra Modi was now '*Gujarat no Nath*' and would remain so unchallenged for thirteen long years when he would resign to take up the prime ministership of India. But before that, he would have to walk through a gauntlet of fire. His ultimate *Agnipariksha*.

▪

In September 2001, the 9/11 terrorist attack in New York brought down the Twin Towers, and two months later, Pakistan-sponsored terrorists attacked the Indian Parliament; they also massacred Sikh men in Kashmir by opening fire. Islamic terrorism was at its peak. General Musharraf, smarting from the defeat in the Kargil battle, had ousted the civilian government in Pakistan and was itching to extract revenge on India.

Pakistan's Inter-Services Intelligence (ISI) was believed to have provided funds and support to elements in Godhra to incite communal violence, exploiting existing tensions in the region.

Since 1927 (when its Deputy Collector, Morarji Desai, had to resign on the charge of being soft on Hindus[11]), Godhra had seen communal riots often (in 1947 and in the 1980s). Godhra was an optimal tinderbox. Modi had just become the Chief Minister.

The demand on the Vajpayee Government to build the Ram temple in Ayodhya at the Babri site was getting intense. Yagnas were being performed, and pilgrims were visiting

11 Umat, Ajay, and Harit Mehta, 'Can Narendra Modi Follow in Morarji Desai's Footsteps?', *The Economic Times*, 10 June 2013, https://tinyurl.com/bdd8335c. Accessed on 10 September 2025.

Ayodhya to participate. A large contingent of pilgrims from Gujarat, after one such yagna, was to return from Ayodhya by the Sabarmati Express.

The plan was to put to death all the pilgrims by setting the Sabarmati Express on fire, when it stopped at Godhra station, in the cover of darkness at night. Fortunately, it was late by four hours, arriving at 7.43 a.m. on 27th February 2002, and the huge mob at the station had slightly thinned down when the train arrived.

Coach S6 was set on fire by a 1500-plus-strong mob, who threw into the compartment burning petrol-soaked rags and electric bulbs filled with acid, after shattering the glass windows with rocks. When the driver tried to pull away, the red chain (emergency brake) was pulled multiple times. The guard tried to release the brake and was stoned by the mob, compelling him to scramble back into his cabin. The fire brigade, which found both its fire trucks sabotaged (removal of the clutch plate and hose tampered), was pelted with stones and severely obstructed. The firemen reached twenty minutes too late. 59 Hindu pilgrims, including 26 women and 12 children, died.

That the burning of the train was a premeditated conspiracy was confirmed by the non-governmental independent Enquiry Commission headed by a highly respected jurist, Justice Debi Singh Tewatia, whose Tewatia Report was published by the Council for International Affairs and Human Rights. Tewatia called it 'not spontaneous, but a clinically planned conspiracy'. This was also confirmed by the Nanavati-Mehta Commission of Enquiry ('terrorist act clinically executed') as well as by the Supreme Court empowered Special Investigative Team (SIT). All these reports were published during 2004-2014 when the Congress was in power at the Centre. All these Commissions found that the burning of the train was not accidental but premeditated. In the weeks before the train burning, there were reports of unusual activity in Godhra—a rise in gun licence applications, sudden purchases of large quantities of petrol, and a visible restlessness among sections of the town's youth. According to the highly respected IPS officer K.P.S. Gill, 'he had definite information hat Pakistan's ISI had ordered Kashmiri militants to sneak into Gujarat to launch terrorist attacks in the state during the recent communal riots.'[12]

On 17th March 2002, the absconding main suspect, Haji Bilal, a Godhra town councillor, was arrested by an anti-terrorist squad at Godhra. Bilal had visited Karachi in Pakistan several times before the burning of the train.

In May 2004, two and a quarter years after the train burning, the UPA came to power in New Delhi, and Lalu Prasad Yadav was appointed as the railway minister. Yadav appointed Justice U.C. Banerjee to investigate the train burning incident. Four months later, Justice Banerjee presented his interim report, which provisionally described the fire as 'accidental', citing a forensic report. Banerjee's findings were challenged in the Gujarat High Court by a victim of the fire, which, in October 2006, quashed the interim report,

---

12 'ISI Planned Terrorist Attack in Gujarat During Riots: Gill.', *The Times of India*, 28 August 2002, https://tinyurl.com/msyanufb. Accessed on 10 September 2025.

ruling that the investigation was 'unconstitutional, illegal, null and void', and was 'a colourable exercise of power with malafide intentions'.[13] The High Court deemed the finding of an accidental fire to be opposed to the prima facie accepted facts on record and directed that the report shall not be tabled in the Parliament.

Coming back to the burning of the train on 27th February 2002. Retaliation was now certain. As expected by the ISI, fire-blowing Hindu militants, along with several from the Muslim side, incited mobs belonging to both communities to riot, in which 790 Muslims and 254 Hindus perished. Most of these rioters were arrested, prosecuted and given long terms of imprisonment.

Narendra Modi had been the Chief Minister for hardly twenty weeks when the train was set on fire. He had zero experience in handling riots or dealing with the police administration. He nevertheless acted instantly. An immediate state-wide curfew was declared, and 217 preventive arrests (137 Hindus, 80 Muslims) of known troublemakers were made. Modi issued written requests to the Government of India to deploy anti-riot police and Central paramilitary forces on the very day of the incident. He was informed that due to Operation Parakram being underway, India had mobilized a massive 500,000 troops at the India-Pakistan border, and no soldiers were immediately available. Modi also realized, to his increasing dismay, that the Gujarat Police

---

13 Dasgupta, Manas, 'Bannerjee Committee illegal: High Court', *The Hindu*, 14 October 2006, https://tinyurl.com/dxtvkw8a. Accessed on 10 September 2025.

was compromised due to the long history of communal polarization in the state.

The Army was ultimately deployed in less than 48 hours after Godhra, and 24 hours after the first death in the riots. This was much faster than riots elsewhere in India. In the anti-Sikh riots following Indira Gandhi's assassination in 1984, no soldier was deployed for four days, and only after thousands had died.

Since Independence, India has witnessed 20,000 riots, small or large, with 440 in Gujarat alone, the state with the most violent history of Hindu-Muslim communal riots. In August 1980, two thousand had died in the Moradabad communal riots. A similar number of deaths took place in Assam in 1983. In Gujarat, in September–October 1969, tensions escalated during the Ramlila festival, leading to widespread violence across Ahmedabad and other districts. Officially, 660 deaths; unofficially, up to 2000 deaths, including 430 Muslims. Muslims lost property worth up to ₹32 million out of a total of ₹42 million worth of property destroyed. In July–August 1985, riots across Gujarat on the reservations issue resulted in 180 deaths. In December 1992–January 1993, widespread communal riots, following the demolition of the Babri Masjid in Ayodhya, saw 227 deaths with 180 in Surat alone, predominantly of Muslims. When the above riots happened, BJP was not in power at the Centre or at the state level.

The Supreme Court of India appointed a highly empowered SIT, which found no evidence that Modi had promoted enmity amongst communities on religious grounds. On the contrary, it noted that Modi had repeatedly appealed for peace and had taken steps for the rehabilitation and medical care of riot victims. The SIT found no delay in deploying the army to control the riot situation and concluded that paramilitary forces were deployed as soon as available. The SIT found no material that Modi or his ministers had interfered with police operations during the VHP-led Gujarat bandh on February 28, 2002, or that Modi had instructed his ministers to interfere with the working of police control rooms.

The findings of the SIT were extensively challenged before the Supreme Court of India, which gave a unanimous judgment on June 24, 2022, upholding the SIT closure report and concurring with the SIT's conclusions that there was no material to support the allegation of a pre-planned conspiracy at the highest level of the state government. The Supreme Court dismissed the appeal, stating that it was devoid of merit and observed that the 'proceedings had been pursuedfor over sixteen years to keep the pot boiling, obviously for an ulterior design'. The Court appreciated the SIT's indefatigable work in challenging circumstances and upheld its approach as objective and thorough.

The English language newspapers, as well as the Western media, true to form, downplayed the burning of the train as an accidental fire due to a cooking gas cylinder or provocation by the pilgrims of the Godhra Muslims on the station; and accused the Modi government of complicity in controlling the riots, refusing to distinguish between Hindu extremists, on the one hand, and the BJP on the other. In the heat of the moment, such inflammatory reporting appeared like gospel and was hungrily lapped up by the Western media, which did not have much presence on the ground.

The palpable bias of this section of the media was exposed, only when years later, the reports of the judicial commissions of enquiry as well as the SIT were made public and brought on record evidence establishing that the burning of the train was a premeditated, well planned operation as also that the Modi government had acted with alacrity in immediately asking for army and paramilitary help. After evaluating evidence and the most elaborate hearings for a decade, the Supreme Court of India had unanimously concluded that no material was found of any complicity at any level of the Modi government.

Never before had the English media so recklessly accused a government of complicity, despite much graver riots, including the pogrom in which thousands of Sikhs died in the aftermath of Indira Gandhi's assassination in 1984 in Delhi, under Rajiv Gandhi's rule. The Marxist historian, Irfan Habib, called this Delhi pogrom, 'mob frenzy'; and the Godhra riots, 'a pogrom'. Habib has been consistently criticized by other respected historians for suppressing inconvenient facts and downplaying both temple destruction and Islamic iconoclasm. Habib, in a preface he wrote to a book on Nehru, fondly recalls how Nehru, a close friend of his father, dropped in at the Habib household in Aligarh unannounced for lunch, in 1942; and how Nehru was instrumental in releasing his blocked passport (due to Habib's communist leanings) to enable young Habib to study abroad.

The disproportionality of the retaliation (790 Muslims and 254 Hindus dead in the riots against 59 Hindu pilgrims burnt alive) was also highlighted, as if such arithmetic was under Modi's control. There was no difference in the anatomy of the Godhra riots and other major riots that had occurred in India over the years. Retaliation has always been disproportionate to the original act of provocation. Peaceful coexistence between Hindus and Muslims is the norm, which, when shattered by a provocation, results in a micro-minority of extremist elements in both communities committing acts of violence, triggering a chain reaction that feeds upon itself. With 79% of the population being Hindus, the Muslim minority often suffers disproportionately.

In the communal riots, which broke out between Hindus and Muslims in the cosmopolitan and liberal minded city of Mumbai in December 1992/January 1993, 900 died, 575 Muslims and 275 Hindus. In an ISI-sponsored retaliation, Mumbai was rocked by 12 coordinated bomb blasts in which 257 died, mostly Hindus. In 2006, Islamic terrorists struck again at Mumbai with pressure cooker bombs planted in the Mumbai suburban trains which exploded in a span of 11 minutes, killing 209 persons, the majority Hindus. In 2008, in the most audacious terrorist act, Pakistani terrorists came by sea to Mumbai and opened indiscriminate fire at six different locations, where in one evening, 166 died, the majority Hindus.

The local police are often biased and compromized, as it was realized by someone as perceptive as Narendra Modi, to his horror, compelling him to ask for immediate army help. Almost in every riot, the sheer presence of the army had ended the violence and mayhem. However, the most serious damage occurs in this interim period before army boots are on the ground.

Reports of enquiry of judicial commissions often take years to come. Before that, the sensationalist reporting of a biased media creates an impression in the public mind, which is so difficult to remove, even when unimpeachable evidence emerges later. This is exactly what happened on a highly exaggerated scale in the case of reporting of the Godhra riots. In 2002, the hostility of the English media against Modi, the Sangh and the BJP was manifold. Under-reporting the burning of the train, focusing heavily on anti-Muslim violence, ignoring the rehabilitation and relief work, instantly pronouncing Modi guilty of complicity, loosely using words like 'pogrom' and 'genocide', were instances of such palpable bias.

There is not an iota of doubt, as history will record, that the English media singled out Narendra Modi for the harshest and the most discriminatory coverage ever given to any chief minister of a state in which such riots had occurred. If this media had an agenda to denigrate Modi, it proved counter-productive in as much as they unwittingly contributed to the accelerating popularity graph of Narendra Modi over the next 23 years. However, they also contributed to the personal anguish, Modi felt, for the first time in his life.

For a man who had only experienced success in every endeavour in his public and political life, Narendra Modi felt utterly helpless in not being able to immediately control the situation. Plagued by self- doubt, he felt personally devastated. The media was braying for his blood. Hindu elements like the VHP (Vishwa Hindu Parishad) and Bajrang Dal, angry that Modi had not prevented their arrest, turned against him. As expected, Congress was demanding his resignation. After much soul-searching, Modi decided to resign.

In 2002, 78-year-old Vajpayee had decided that his deputy Prime Minister, Advani, would be the PM candidate of the BJP at the next elections in 2004. Vajpayee was constantly trying to fend off pressure from his party and the Sangh to construct a Ram temple at Ayodhya. At that point of time, Vajpayee did not want his legacy as a poet and a statesman with moderate views, to be besmirched in any manner.

It is in this frame of mind that Vajpayee came to Ahmedabad in April 2002 and addressed a video recorded press conference along with Modi. When Vajpayee was asked whether he had any advice for the Chief Minister, he replied that that the Chief Minister must follow his *Rajdharma* and that Vajpayee was himself following the same, as the Prime Minister. He elaborated that it meant that a ruler must not make any distinction between his subjects on any religious or communal grounds. Thereupon, Modi promptly said that he had always followed such *Rajdharma*. Vajpayee concurred and said that 'I am confident that Narendra *bhai* is indeed following the *Rajdharma*'.

Modi publicly offered his letter of resignation, to the National Executive of the BJP at Goa. Modi did not want the image of Gujarat to be sullied anymore. More importantly, he did not want the BJP to suffer. Modi addressed the meet for hardly two minutes, in what was described as *Alipta Bhava*, a totally detached state of mind.

As soon as he finished speaking, the entire gathering was on its feet, with shouts of 'No! No! Never!' Modi's resignation was summarily rejected.

A few months later, on 24th September 2002, ISI openly struck again at Gujarat when two heavily armed terrorists opened fire on the Akshardham Temple in Gandhinagar, killing 27, including children, all of them Hindus. Commandos from New Delhi were rapidly airlifted and shot dead the terrorists. There was not a single communal incident following this massacre.

Narendra Modi would ensure that there was no serious or major communal riot during his 13 years as Gujarat chief minister. Muslims of India, increasingly voted for the BJP reaching its peak of support in the 2012 Gujarat elections, realizing that Narendra Modi is a Hindu nationalist, but neither is he anti-Muslim nor is he a communalist.

One can well understand, why the angered Shankarsinh Vaghela recklessly and absurdly accused the VHP itself of engineering the train burning at Godhra to provoke riots against the Muslims; how is one to understand the prejudice of an Indian historian, Ramachandra Guha, who, in the third edition of his book, *India After Gandhi*, published in 2023, when the reports of the Commissions of Enquiry, including the Tewatia report, findings of the SIT, the Nanavati Mehta Commission Report, and the Supreme Court judgement confirming the SIT findings, had all been published, described the Godhra incident as follows:

> 'On their way back home by train, these kar sevaks got into a fight with Muslim vendors at the Godhra

> railway station. The vendors were asked to chant slogans in homage to Lord Ram; when they refused, their beards were pulled. Word of the altercation spread; young men from the Muslim neighbourhood outside the station joined in. The kar sevaks clambered back into the train, which started moving even as stones were being thrown. However, the train stopped on the outskirts of the station, a fire broke out in one of its coaches.'[14]

Guha's account describes the riots in detail but does not have even a whisper about any of the above reports of enquiry or the Supreme Court judgement exonerating Modi.

Then Guha unwittingly reveals the reason for his bias in the following words:

> 'As an Indian citizen committed to pluralism, I remain deeply worried about the growing demonization of my Muslim compatriots, about the transformation of a democratic and secular republic into a Hindu majoritarian state.'[15]

Gujarat became the laboratory for the transformative model of all-round development of the country flawlessly executed by Narendra Modi, who went on to win three assembly elections for the BJP, in 2002, 2007 and 2012, with consummate ease.

---

14 Guha, Ramchandra, 'Chapter 26: Rights and Riots', *India After Gandhi: A History (3rd Edition, Revised and Updated)*, Picador India, Delhi, 2023, pp. 601-628

15 Ibid.

Modi had walked through the gauntlet of fire and emerged unscathed. It was time now for the Gujarat no Nath to transform his state.

CHAPTER FIVE

The Elite's Allergy

A SECTION OF THE intellectual elite in India has just not been able to decode Narendra Modi. Even after he became Chief Minister of Gujarat for a fourth time, they believed that his political fortunes were limited to being a strong regional leader. In early 2013, despite the rapid emergence of Modi as a national leader, they were confident that he would not be named as the prime ministerial candidate of the BJP. It was only when the momentum generated by him during the 2014 campaign looked unstoppable that the elite became distinctly nervous. Some declared that they would migrate if Narendra Modi became the prime minister. None did.

The 2014 victory of the NDA (BJP) was regarded by them as an aberration, a one-time mandate due to anger against the non-performance of the UPA during its second term. The elite were skeptical that the NDA was unlikely to win again. Hence, in 2019, they were rejuvenated by their belief that the BJP would lose. Instead, the BJP secured a record majority and required no coalition. In 2024, due to a setback to the BJP on the results day, their hopes were enlivened momentarily, only to subside.

What the elite fails to appreciate is that Modi has triggered a structural change in the dynamics of the political landscape of India, which ensures that, in the medium term, the probability of dislodging a highly disciplined party promoting a nationalist agenda, is minimal.

To use a rather insensitive analogy, Modi is like an atomic bomb that has fallen on the elite's cherished notions and ideas. Ivory towers and cocoons rudely disturbed, they cannot digest that a tea vendor's seemingly unsophisticated son, an RSS *pracharak*, from the backwaters of Gujarat, has become the Prime Minister of India for a third successive term. The elite, which claims to be dispassionate, actually bristles with prejudice against Modi. The reasons for the allergy are many. However, prior to dissecting their mindset, let us first define what is meant by the expression, the Indian intellectual elite, in the present context.

Political or religious propagandists of any hue, having an agenda, are obviously to be excluded. The elite, referred to here, comprises mostly highly accomplished individuals, usually with integrity and ethics in personal life, with no overt connections to any political party or organization. It comprises of academicians, historians, biographers, lawyers, and media persons. Of course, not all of them nurse such prejudice.

A typical profile of a 'Modi allergic' is a person educated in the English medium (mostly in acclaimed boarding schools in the hill stations or famed schools in the metropolis, with a foreign degree in the liberal arts thrown in) from an upper middle-class professional family, with centre-of-left liberal leanings and atheistic agnostic views on religion. Dry rationalists, whose ability to intuitively grasp issues is often blunted. They wear what they incorrectly term as secularism on their sleeve. Many of them are secretly condescending about those tutored in the vernacular medium who cannot speak King's English.

The elite have been brought up on a staple diet of historical narratives of post-Independence India, which skilfully gloss over all the acts of commission and omission of the so-called secular leaders while highlighting the sins of those they dub as Hindu communalists.

Painful though it is, reference has to be made, in some detail, to the historical backdrop, which has shaped the mindset and approach of this elite. It begins with the Partition of India and Mahatma Gandhi.

The Partition was heart-wrenching for the Mahatma and shattered his dream of a United India, where Hindus and Muslims peacefully coexisted. However, the Congress leadership under Nehru was willing to compromise in the interest of gaining Independence, and the Mahatma had to most reluctantly agree.

Post independence, the Congress, in a political master stroke, could have channelized a part of the Hindu nationalist fervour, had Gandhi agreed to select the iron-willed Vallabhbhai Patel instead of Jawaharlal Nehru as the first prime minister of India.

The elite continued to prefer the suave, urbane, red-rose-in-the-sherwani Nehru, to the stoic and no-nonsense Patel. JRD Tata, the highly respected outspoken patriarch of the Tata Group, in an interview with Rajiv Mehrotra, after saying that he loved and admired Nehru, candidly admitted that Nehru knew little about economics, and was not even interested in discussing the subject with Tata, instead looking out of the window in his garden, where there was a giant panda. Tata added that had Patel been the younger man and chosen prime minister, things could have been quite different.[16]

Deep down, the elite believed that Patel was a closet sympathizer of Hindu nationalism. The elite of those days, also viewed with distaste the tactics of Patel in bringing nearly five hundred Indian Princes forcibly into the Indian Republic. Many of the displaced royalty later joined hands with the pro American right wing Indian intellectuals to form the Swatantra Party which was highly vocal but did not achieve much politically. Years later, Indira Gandhi, would treat some of this royalty even more roughly by unceremoniously throwing them behind bars, during the Emergency.

Jawaharlal Nehru endeared himself to the elite with his lyrical talk of 'tryst with destiny', in a clipped English accent at midnight when Independence was ushered in. Nehru was an honest, sensitive, and cultured individual who would have made a great ambassador for the country at the United Nations. The elite felt he was one of them. He was, after all a class act, almost minor royalty. He undoubtedly enjoyed

---

16 'Tata Group', *JRD Tata: In Conversation | Heritage*, Tata Group, July 2019, https://tinyurl.com/2jvez624. Accessed on 10 September 2025.

oodles of goodwill and affection of the masses. Those were the days of polite newspapers, government-controlled radio, very low literacy rates, and disciplined parliamentarians.

Indira Gandhi was a conundrum for the elite. Initially, they preferred her chiffon-clad grace, sophistication and softness to the other Congress politicians who were considered crude with their Gandhi caps and dhotis. Morarji Desai, Indira's long-time nemesis, though recognized as an excellent administrator and scrupulously honest, was mocked by the elite for non-issues like his liquor prohibition policies and treating urine as a nature cure. Desai was certainly not one of them, even though he was a star of the reputed Civil Service from which he resigned, following allegations that as deputy collector, he had been soft on the Hindus during the Godhra communal riots in 1927-28. A familiar-sounding charge indeed.

Indira undoubtedly made a far better prime minister than her father. The nation saluted her when she stood up to the Nixon-Kissinger arm-twisting during the 1970-71 campaign to liberate Bangladesh. She had verve, panache and a native cunning. However, she believed that the Constitution and the Courts were the biggest roadblock towards socioeconomic progress, and somewhere deep down, she had genuine contempt for the system.

The elite's love affair with Indira Gandhi soured badly when she exposed her dictatorial and authoritarian side, by declaring the Emergency. Cornered by the judgment of the Allahabad High Court, in an electoral malpractice case, which prohibited her from holding public office for six years, and the growing nationwide agitation led by the venerated Jayaprakash Narayan, she imprisoned every possible leader of the opposition, including Narayan, Advani, Vajpayee and Morarji Desai. A Censor from the Government of India was posted in the office of every large newspaper, civil liberties were suspended, and dissent was suppressed. She launched the most systematic assault on the Constitution of India, by advocating a committed judiciary and a committed bureaucracy. 'India is Indira and Indira is India', declared the Congress President, Dev Kant Barua, an Assamese poet, who became lyrical about his Queen. Indira's recidivist son, Sanjay Gandhi, went amok, bulldozing slums and forcibly sterilizing people (more than a crore of men were sterilized), violating the human rights of both Hindus and Muslims.

What suddenly prompted her in early 1977 to revoke the Emergency and declare national elections is still a matter of debate. Some said she was unable to withstand the criticism of the Western media that she was a dictator. Others said that she did not want Nehru's daughter to go down in history as an autocrat. Some felt that she was fed up with her problem child, Sanjay, who would die soon after she regained power in 1980, while trying to attempt an aerobatic manoeuvre in a glider wearing Kolhapuri chappals. Maybe, she delusionally believed the Intelligence Bureau reports that she would be re-elected; or was missing the mass adulation she so enjoyed. Maybe the forces which shape India's destiny were back in play.

For the first time, the elite including the Western media had to grudgingly accept the stellar role of the Sangh in opposing the Emergency to salvage civil liberties, and thereafter vigorously campaigning for the newly formed Janata party in which had merged the Bharatiya Jana Sangh, the ideological child of the Sangh.

In a low-profile manner, during those decades, the Sangh continued to build a formidable, disciplined organization spread all over the country and quietly did heartwarming relief work during natural disasters, such as famine and earthquakes. In 1979, when a dam breached in Morbi, Gujarat, resulting in the loss of thousands of lives, Narendra Modi, as a 29-year-old *pracharak*, personally picked up numerous swollen and disfigured corpses, and cremated them.

Out of the 295 seats, the Janata Party secured in the 1977 election, 96 seats were won by the faction, which was earlier the Bhartiya Jana Sangh. This was in no small measure attributable to the Sangh. The faction had two key cabinet posts occupied by its leaders, Atal Bihari Vajpayee and Lal Krishna Advani, as Minister for External Affairs and Minister for Information & Broadcasting, respectively. The elite kept a wary eye on these two ministers, who, despite their capability, due to the complex internal political dynamics of the Janata Party, could not leave their imprimatur on this short-lived government.

The elite initially had a rollicking love affair with Rajiv Gandhi when he swept to power with a hitherto unparalleled majority of 414 out of 543 seats in the 1984 elections in the sympathy wave following the assassination of his mother, Indira. Jan Sangh, now called the Bharatiya Janata Party or BJP, was decimated and managed to secure only two seats.

Amiable, benign, handsome, soft spoken, and a saint as

compared to his adjective-defying late brother Sanjay, Rajiv, a professional pilot with a penchant for technology, initially appeared like a God-sent to the elite. He ticked all their boxes for being India's prime minister.

This love affair ended abruptly when the Swedish Radio on 16th April 1987 exposed a bribery scandal involving a Swedish arms manufacturer, Bofors AB, from whom the Rajiv Gandhi government had purchased Howitzer guns in 1986. Bofors admitted, in writing to the Swedish National Audit Bureau, paying bribes totalling USD 16,000,000 to Indian politicians and defence officials. Even though Rajiv was not legally indicted, his role in allegedly slowing the investigation and in the mysterious disappearance of Ottavio Quattrocchi, the key middleman of Italian origin with close links, affected his reputation and led to the defeat of the Congress in the 1989 elections (from 414 seats to 197). V.P. Singh, his finance minister, rebelled and became Prime Minister. Bofors became synonymous with corruption in India. The intelligentsia's disillusionment with the Congress grew.

The 1989–1999 politically turbulent and destabilizing decade saw the end of Congress dominance, the start of the coalition era, and the BJP emerging as a national force. The short-lived V.P. Singh and Chandra Shekhar coalition governments led to fresh elections in 1991. During the campaigning, Rajiv Gandhi's assassination by Sri Lanka's LTTE led to a return of the Congress on a sympathy wave. P. V. Narasimha Rao ran a minority government skillfully and managed to finish his full five-year term as Prime Minister. In the 1996 elections, the BJP emerged as the single largest party and Vajpayee became Prime Minister, to resign only after 13 days, due to loss of his majority in the House. Weak coalition governments of H.D. Deve Gowda and I.K. Gujral collapsed after Congress played hide-and-seek with its external support.

In the 1999 elections, the BJP-led NDA won a clear majority, and Prime Minister Vajpayee lasted his full term of five years. Due to the compulsion of the coalition government he led, he projected himself as being above narrow party lines. The elite naturally did not mind him.

The last prime minister before Modi, Dr Manmohan Singh, so appropriately called the accidental Prime Minister, was in stark contrast to Narendra Modi. A soft-spoken Oxbridge-educated economist and bureaucrat, he was unabashedly the proxy for the Italian-origin Sonia Gandhi, who prudently chose not to be the prime minister. Competent, honest, learned, apolitical and gentlemanly, Dr Singh was the first PM who displayed not the slightest emotional fervour for the job. In the closing stages of his second five-year term in office, he was tired, listless, speechless and appeared lost.

It must be said to his credit, though, that he refused to sanction or be a party to any trumped-up prosecution or legal action, which his aggressive and increasingly desperate party men encouraged him to take against Modi, to prevent the latter from becoming the prime minister. During a parliamentary debate in 2021, Modi acknowledged the decency and work ethic of Dr Singh.

For long in a state of denial, when Narendra Modi finally did become a *fait accompli*, the elite was confident that New Delhi was no Gandhinagar, and Modi, a first-time member of Parliament ever to straight-away become Prime Minister, may have lorded over his native Gujarat, but would soon discover that governing India was altogether a different cup of tea. Finding his way through the maze of bureaucracy in North Block or dealing with other countries would prove to be beyond Modi's competence. His administrative experience as the chief minister of Gujarat for thirteen years would prove inadequate for running the Central government. Neither Western powers nor Islamic countries approved of him. He did not speak good English and was unsophisticated. His radicalism will terribly backfire on him. Narendra Modi's prime ministership was a disaster in the making. The elite waited with bated breath for Modi to fail.

Ironically, some of Modi's committed supporters too were apprehensive as to how he would perform. A few of the BJP's own senior leaders, fuming at being bypassed for the top job, were secretly hoping that he did not succeed. The Western media was not far behind during the 2014 campaign, and even after he was elected, there were highly critical editorials and articles about him. *TIME* magazine headlined: Modi means business, but can he lead India? *The Economist* of London, on the eve of the election, ran an editorial titled: Can anyone stop Narendra Modi?[17]

However, Bharat Bhagya Vidhata and Modi's Jagat Janani apparently had other plans. Each apprehension proved incorrect. After the very first hundred days in office, the wind had gone out of the sails of the elite.

---

17 'Can Anyone Stop Narendra Modi?', *The Economist*, 5 April 2014, https://tinyurl.com/vkhyc2hz. Accessed on 10 September 2025.

In those hundred days, Modi reduced bureaucratic layers, enforced biometric attendance for government officers, and launched the Swachh Bharat Mission on Gandhi's birth anniversary. He inaugurated the Jan Dhan Yojana with 15 million bank accounts opened on Day One, announced policy initiatives on industrial corridors, smart cities and broadband connectivity in villages. Initiated measures to increase the flow of Foreign Direct Investment and operationalized an SIT for recovering black money in offshore accounts of resident Indians. Countries vied with each other to invite him for a visit, including the ones which had earlier denied him a visa. Despite such personal affront, Modi warmly accepted America's invitation to visit.

Upon completion of 12 months of his tenure, Narendra Modi had record approval ratings in surveys conducted by independent international service providers, showing that 87% of Indians held a favourable view of Modi, with 68% rating him 'very favourable', and 93% approving of his Government.

In July 2025, according to the authoritative Morning Consult Survey, Narendra Modi enjoyed the highest approval rating among all democratically elected leaders globally, towering heads and shoulders over everybody, with an approval rating of 75%, after 11 years continuously in office.

The Economist finally received an answer to its question and had to grudgingly record its admiration for Modi, time and again. Modi won the *TIME* magazine online readers' poll for 'Person of the Year', securing millions of votes, surpassing Obama and Trump.

Without taking away from Modi's extraordinary abilities and commitment, this superhuman performance against all odds would not have been possible without the continuing divine protection, which Narendra Modi receives from the forces that govern India's destiny.

Whatever may be their virtues and merits, the elite have consistently been allergic, not only to Narendra Modi, but also to the likes of Vallabhbhai Patel and Morarji Desai. The elite cannot digest a rustic son of the soil who knows the pulse of the people. Amongst the very short-lived prime ministers of India, V.P. Singh and I.K. Gujral were acceptable to the elite but not Charan Singh or Chandra Shekhar or Deve Gowda. A person who has not received a classic English education or who speaks with a vernacular accent is looked down upon. Not one of us, they think. However, after 1992, the reasons for the elite's allergy were different.

The elite believes that while no decent Hindu bears animus against Indian Muslims or supports any extremist group causing harm to any innocent Muslim man, woman or child, increasingly many Hindus and even other non-Muslim communities harbour social prejudice against the Muslims. A strong nationalist leader, who apprehends the elite, may build on this in-built prejudice, making the minorities feel insecure. Ever since the demolition of the Babri Masjid in 1992 and the subsequent groundswell in Hindu nationalism, the elite has become more apprehensive of any nationalist party or leader coming into power and authority.

When an overconfident BJP surprisingly lost the 2004 elections, the elite regarded it as a rejection of Hindu nationalism by the electorate. Five years later, in 2009, despite widespread discontent about a worsening economy and corruption scandals of the Congress-led UPA, when the BJP performed worse than in 2004, the elite concluded that the BJP was rejected due to its PM candidate Advani's role in the demolition of the Babri and its Hindutva agenda.

The elite was wrong in its reasoning. Both these elections were lost by the BJP for multiple other reasons; primarily due to the feeling of the rural electorate that the BJP was an urban party for the privileged, not having extensive social welfare schemes like the UPA. While Advani had a clean image, at 82 years of age, several pre-election surveys showed that he was perceived as being somewhat inflexible and unable to emotionally connect with the younger electorate. Also, despite several corruption scandals of the UPA, the squeaky-clean personal image of Dr Manmohan Singh greatly helped the UPA to win. The elite thus became sanguine that Hindu nationalists cannot capture power unless they were in a highly diluted coalition, like the government in 1999 under the Cola Lite version of Vajpayee.

Narendra Modi, as a serious prime ministerial contender, was therefore on nobody's radar in 2009.

At times, when greater forces wish to propel someone suddenly to power, the public consciousness is altered to become oblivious to the possibility of such a person's rise. The punch in the solar plexus has to land suddenly.

The elite and the political pundits did not even contemplate Modi ever being the BJP's PM face, leave alone becoming PM. Had the BJP leadership itself been asked the question at that time, they would have themselves perhaps ruled it out. Despite two consecutive electoral defeats, Advani was still aspiring.

The elite was shocked out of its wits when, in June 2013, the BJP announced Modi, the only eminently winnable candidate, as the head of its 2014 Election Campaign Committee. Advani resigned all his party positions.

Ten weeks later, the rising swell of its ground root cadre, who sensed victory, led the BJP leadership to announce Modi as its PM candidate. This proved to be a masterstroke. The elite gulped in disbelief. Its worst nightmare had come true. For the next eight months, with diminishing hope, the elite thought that surely Narendra Modi could not be the prime minister of India. Disconnected with ground realities, the elite failed to appreciate that the country was desperately yearning for Narendra Modi to end the sleeping beauty act of Dr Manmohan Singh.

The elite simply cannot distinguish between Hindu cultural nationalism, on the one hand, and rabid communalism targeting a minority, on the other. The shadow of religion must fall nowhere near the State, believes the elite. Even if the 2002 riots had never happened, they would have still been antithetical to Narendra Modi. It is only now, after Modi's third electoral success, that the elite has grudgingly realized that Bharat wants Modi.

The elite has still not realized that even beyond Modi, India wants its prime minister to be a nationalist and that the emergence of the Hindu nation as a civilizational and cultural way of life is inevitable.

They also do not realize that, ironically, the minorities feel most secure and safe under such a dispensation. This is reflected in the BJP's increasing share of the Muslim vote in recent elections.

A nationalist leader who worships Lord Rama in a temple, meditates in Kanyakumari, and fasts during Navratri, embarrasses them. The truth is that this section of the elite is increasingly in a hopeless micro-minority in the thought space of the country.

CHAPTER SIX

A Way of Life

IT IS DIFFICULT to believe that Vinayak Savarkar was admittedly an atheist. He dreamt of a civilizational, cultural and ethnic Hindu nation, not a theological one. Neither the Sangh nor the BJP wants India to be a theocratic State like Saudi Arabia or Pakistan or Iran. Or even a non-theocratic country having an official religion like Jewish Israel, Shinto Buddhist Japan or Buddhist Thailand. Cultural nationalism, not religious rule, constitutes the notion of a *Hindu Rashtra*. *Rashtra*, in this context, is not to be translated as nation—a political territorial unit. It is a way of life which ensures justice to all in society without discrimination on grounds of religion or caste, or language.

In 1976, during the Emergency, with most opposition leaders in jail, Indira Gandhi amended the Constitution to add the word secular to the Preamble. The prevailing constitutional position was not altered in any manner by the addition of this word. This was clearly a cosmetic exercise to portray a part of the imprisoned opposition as communal right-wing reactionaries. Despite this, in none of its election manifestoes, the BJP say that it seeks to amend the Constitution to delete the word.

Across the political spectrum in India, there is unanimity that the State shall not discriminate on grounds of religion and that all religions shall be treated equally under the law. It is a tribute to the maturity of the Indian polity that this consensus prevails, despite India being squeezed on either side by hostile Islamic theocracies, Pakistan, and now Bangladesh.

This position is cast in stone in the Constitution in the form of Fundamental Rights under Article 15 and Article 25 and has always been upheld by the Supreme Court of India. As an eminent philosopher and a former President of India, Dr S Radhakrishnan believed that secular does not mean irreligious; it means to respect all religions.

Of course, the nationalists do not want that in the name of secularism, there is either appeasement of religious minorities, or downplaying or condoning terrorism. That is pseudo-secularism or unequal treatment under the law, says the Sangh. Underneath a lofty garb, the Congress made secularism an instrument to capture vote banks.

The dubious credit of successfully implementing such policies for the first time, goes to a politician called Madhav Singh Solanki, Chief Minister of Gujarat four times, who devised a formula known as KHAM (Kshatriya, Harijan, Adivasi and Muslim) then constituting nearly 57% of the Gujarat state population, who received additional benefits of social welfare schemes and other economic largesse from the State, to induce them to switch their political loyalties to the Congress. Solanki's sinister arithmetic resulted in the Congress getting a record 3/4 majority in the Gujarat legislative assembly. Unfortunately, these policies also resulted in a flare-up of ugly communal and caste violence in the state.

Emboldened by his success, five years later, as a pre-poll inducement, Solanki tried to implement a policy of reservation of government jobs to the extent of nearly 50% for KHAM. The Indian Army had to be called to quell the riots, which followed, in which more than 179 persons perished, with 6000 rendered homeless. Years later, Solanki, a close confidant of Rajiv Gandhi, had to resign as India's foreign minister after admitting that he had tried to influence the Swiss government to slow down its investigation into the bribes received in Swiss bank accounts, in the Bofors corruption scandal.

Variations of the KHAM experiment were tried by the Congress, then on a national scale. In the name of secularism, the Congress practiced the policy of positive discrimination or affirmative action, which was not religion-neutral and not contemplated by the Indian Constitution.

Although the then 34-year-old Modi would become Chief Minister of Gujarat only seventeen years later, he resolved that he would never base his electoral arithmetic on caste or religion and will stick to the mantra of equal economic development. Modi has not deviated from this resolve.

■

The concept of a Hindu Rashtra finds its genesis in the Vedic Age (1500-500 BCE) when the Vedas and the Upanishads came into being. However, the golden age of Hindu culture was during the Gupta Empire's rule (320-550 CE) when Sanskrit became the official language, Hindu Vaishnavite temples were constructed, and Ayurveda flourished. Later, the *Mahabharata* and the Puranas expounded the idea that India was a sacred land of holy rivers like the Ganga and Yamuna and the ancient pilgrim centres in the Himalayas.

In modern times, Savarkar, in 1923, published his magnum opus: *Hindutva: Who is a Hindu?* distinguishing between Hinduism as a religion and Hindutva as a political and cultural ideology, a way of life. A Hindu is one who recognizes India, both as his fatherland, and also the holy land, wrote Savarkar.

Koenraad Elst, an Indologist from Belgium, concluded that the idea of a Hindu Rashtra is not about establishing a theocratic State. It is about recognizing India's civilizational roots in Hindu culture. India's identity has been historically shaped by Hinduism, and hence, a nation that acknowledges this heritage is more authentic and cohesive. Elst believes that secularism in India has often been a facade that undermines the nation's true identity by promoting a false sense of neutrality, which actually marginalizes Hindu culture.[18]

Seventy-two years later, the Supreme Court of India, echoing Savarkar, observed in an election malpractice case (Prabhu v. Kunte, 1995) that Hinduism was not religious dogma; it was a cultural ethos; 'a way of life'. While the Constitution ensures that India cannot be a theocratic State,

---

18 Elst, Koenraad. 'Guha's Golwalkar', *Koenraad Elst Blogspot*, 4 November 2016, https://tinyurl.com/3uc2cp7n. Accessed on 10 September 2025.

the Constitution cannot come in the way of a civilizational and cultural notion of a Hindu Rashtra.

For the Sangh and the BJP, the notion of a Hindu Rashtra required the implementation of their long-promised agenda, comprising ending the special constitutional status of Kashmir, reconstruction of the Ram Mandir at Ayodhya, the enactment of the Uniform Civil Code, and providing shelter and citizenship to persecuted Indian minorities abroad.

■

Kashmir, a centre of Shaivism, had strong Hindu roots since Vedic times. This changed in the 14th century when a Sufi saint, Syed Ali Hamdani, led a wave of conversions to Islam, and the Shah Mir dynasty began to rule Kashmir. In the dying years of the 14th century, Sultan Sikandar of this dynasty unleashed iconoclasm to desecrate Hindu idols and temples, impose Jizya tax on Hindus and banned the application of tilak on the forehead. Ultimately, to escape persecution, Hindus fled the Valley, changing its entire demography.

Historians have recorded seven distinct waves of Hindu exoduses, fleeing from persecution, upto 1819, when the cycle turned once again, with Maharaja Ranjit Singh conquering Kashmir from the Afghans, which led to the Dogra Dynasty ruling it. The last of the Maharajas of this dynasty was the unfairly pilloried Hari Singh (enthroned, 1925), around whom the saga of Article 370, which conferred a special constitutional status upon Kashmir, is entwined.

A cunningly crafted narrative, now demonstrated to be palpably false, (by documentary evidence available in the public domain) laid the blame for the Kashmir situation entirely on Maharaja Hari Singh. While the truth is that it was Jawaharlal Nehru, himself of Kashmiri descent, and his inexplicable obsessive support for Sheikh Abdullah, which was primarily responsible for all that Kashmir suffered and continues to bleed till today.

In 1945, addressing the Annual Session of the National Conference, Sheikh Abdullah's political party, Nehru warned the Kashmiri Hindus: 'If non-Muslims want to live in Kashmir, they should join the National Conference or say goodbye to the country.'[19]

After Hari Singh arrested Abdullah on 20th May 1946, Nehru developed a paranoid dislike for the Maharaja. This was aggravated when Nehru was himself detained on the border of Kashmir, to prevent him from defending Abdullah at the latter's trial.

Jawaharlal Nehru's aide documented his reaction to being detained, describing how Nehru forcefully stamped his foot on the ground and declared that in the future, the Maharaja of Kashmir would have to repent and apologize to him for the disrespect shown to the President-elect of the Indian National Congress.[20]

---

19 Vashisht, Sunanda, 'Opinion: When Nehru Threatened Wary Kashmiri Pandits to Join National Conference', *News18*, 23 August 2023, https://tinyurl.com/45z8mswj. Accessed on 10 September 2025.

20 Mishra, Akhilesh. 'Why Nehru & Not Maharaja Hari Singh Was Responsible for Delay in Accession of Jammu-Kashmir', *Organiser*,

Hari Singh always wanted to join the Indian Union, as admitted by Nehru himself in the Lok Sabha in 1952. However, Nehru was in no hurry. He said, 'The advice we gave to both (Maharaja and Abdullah) was that Kashmir is a special case, and it would not be right or proper to try to rush things there.' More shockingly, Nehru told the Lok Sabha, 'Even if the Maharaja and his Government want to accede to India, we would like something much more, that is popular approval.'[21]

Later, Nehru added one more condition for accession: first, release Abdullah from jail, only then can we talk about accession to India. On 25th November 1947, Nehru again told the Parliament: 'We did not want a mere accession from the top, but an association in accordance with the will of her people.'[22]

Even Lord Mountbatten, Governor-General of India, documented Nehru's single-minded and rather desperate focus on Abdullah's release. Nehru's demands for agreeing to the accession of Kashmir to India continued to increase. He wrote to Mahajan, Prime Minister of Maharaja Hari Singh, on 21st October 1947: 'Sheikh Abdullah, who is obviously the most popular person in Kashmir, might be asked to form such a (provisional) government.'

In the meantime, the Pakistani Army invaded Kashmir and was about to reach Srinagar. A desperate Maharaja Hari

---

11 December 2023, https://tinyurl.com/yc2f-8c6. Accessed on 10 September 2025.

21 Ibid.

22 Ibid.

Singh accepted all of Nehru's demands and made Sheikh Abdullah the Prime Minister. The accession was finally signed on 26th October 1947. Hari Singh was instantly banished from Kashmir. He would stay for the rest of his life in Bombay. Only his ashes would return to his former Kingdom in 1961. His son, Karan Singh, was appointed Regent and later as *Sardar-e-Riyasat* by Nehru. Later, Dr Karan Singh, a formidable Vedanta scholar, became a minister in Indira Gandhi's cabinet.

After the accession, Pakistan's Prime Minister, Liaquat Ali Khan, was flabbergasted to receive a cable from Nehru on 28th October 1947, stating that the 'accession was subject to the decision of the Kashmiri people'. In other words, it was conditional.

Nehru did not stop there. In October–November 1947, he wrote to world leaders reiterating his commitment to a plebiscite by the people of Kashmir to ascertain their wishes. Further, he took the Kashmir issue (he called it a 'dispute') to the UN. Kashmir was no longer an internal matter of India. Till today, Pakistan relies upon this Indian stand in the UN and other international fora.

When Abdullah showed his true colours six years later, by challenging the accession itself and advocating Kashmiri Independence, Nehru was forced by his cabinet colleagues to put Abdullah in jail, where he would remain for nearly 11 years until his release a few days before Nehru's death. Abdullah's jail term was spent entirely in spacious Government bungalows in the hill stations of Ooty and Kodaikanal in Tamil Nadu and similar places of scenic beauty in Kashmir, where he was provided with cooks, servants and other facilities. Abdullah wept openly and uncontrollably when informed of Nehru's passing.

Wily Jinnah invited Nehru to Lahore to discuss the Kashmir issue. Nehru wanted to accept Jinnah's invite, with Patel opposing it because it meant appeasing Pakistan, the aggressor. It was left to Gandhi to resolve, who advised against spurning an opportunity for peace, and sent the British Governor General Mountbatten, on behalf of India, to Pakistan, as Nehru felt ill. Abdullah's demands for autonomy were tamely conceded by Mountbatten, who was perhaps in a hurry to go back to England with his wife, Edwina.

General Cariappa and General Thimmaiyya of the Indian Army were confident of throwing the Pakistani invaders out of the portion of Kashmir they had occupied, but Nehru decided to take the matter to the UN, and a ceasefire came into force. Had Nehru continued to let the Indian Army fight Pakistan in 1948 and not allowed Pakistan to occupy a part of Kashmir, many Indian lives would have been saved over the decades.

Drafting the constitutional provisions to grant autonomy to Kashmir was delegated by Nehru, unbelievable though it may sound, to the former prime minister of Princely Kashmir, Gopalaswamy Ayyangar, a close confidant of both Nehru and Abdullah. Abdullah, by repeatedly changing his stance on the draft, terrorized Ayyangar to widen the scope of the Article to give extremely wide autonomy to Kashmir. Abdullah, for all practical purposes, almost had a veto power over the draft, due to his special friend, Nehru.

While Patel handled the accession of all other Princely States, Nehru made it clear that Kashmir's accession would be overseen only by him. Patel took a backseat. When Patel finally read the fine print, it was too late. It had already been passed by the Constituent Assembly. All he could do was send an angry letter to Ayyangar. Patel wrote that he realized that, after all, Ayyangar was acting in accordance with Nehru's instructions. Thus, Article 370, wider than ever intended, was born.

J&K now had its own Constitution, its own Prime Minister and its own flag. Indian citizens required a permit to enter the state, as if it were foreign territory. Even the Supreme Court's jurisdiction was limited only to hearing appeals.

Was this due to Nehru's Kashmiri descent and his great sympathy for ascertaining the wishes of the people of Kashmir, or his ambition to be seen as a statesman on the international stage or capitulation to his special friend, is anybody's guess. Pakistan Occupied Kashmir (PoK) remains the biggest security risk to India.

Instead of Nehru, had Patel been left to deal with Kashmir, in the same way as he had tamed the five hundred other Princes of India, much conflict would have been avoided. No wonder Narendra Modi erected the Statue of Unity in Gujarat to commemorate the lifelong Congressman, Sardar Patel.

Article 370, declared to be 'temporary and transitional' by Ayyangar in the Constituent Assembly, would last for 72 years. Article 370 thus was a wart on the face of national integrity. It had to be cauterized.

Dr Syama Prasad Mookerjee, the founder of the Bharatiya Jana Sangh, was passionately opposed to Article 370. Hindu nationalists recited Mookerjee's slogan with great pride, which said '*Ek desh mein do vidhan, do Pradhan, do nishan, nahin chalenge*' (One nation cannot have two Constitutions, two Prime Ministers and two flags). In May 1953, Dr Mookerjee decided to enter Kashmir, as a mark of protest, without the required permit from the Kashmir Government.

Sheikh Abdullah was Prime Minister and Kashmir was bristling with tension. On May 10, 1953, Dr Mookerjee was arrested after he crossed the border into the Kashmir state and was detained in a small cottage converted into a sub-jail, near Dal Lake in Srinagar. Although it was known to Prime Minister Sheikh Abdullah's government that Mookerjee had a leg injury, he was made to climb a long flight of stairs to reach the cottage. On June 20th, he was administered streptomycin, despite having informed the doctor that he was allergic to it. According to a biographer of Mookerjee, Tathagata Roy, Mookerjee was also administered some unknown powder alleged to be a painkiller. Dr Mookerjee requested the Superintendent of the jail to inform his relatives about his illness. However, no such intimation was given. On 22nd June, his health deteriorated severely. It was only on 23rd June that he was taken to the gynaecological ward in the state hospital. Before Dr Mookerjee's assistants could rush to the hospital, 13 days before his 52nd birthday, Dr Mookerjee died.

Abdullah's government did not carry out any post-mortem. Mookerjee's mother, Jagmaya Devi, asked Nehru to initiate a detailed probe into the suspicious death of her son, a request that Nehru denied. None other than a leader of the stature of former Prime Minister Vajpayee alleged in 2004 that Dr Mookerjee was killed as a part of a conspiracy between the Central Government and the J&K Government. Vajpayee alleged that it was decided that Dr Mookerjee should be allowed to enter J&K but not be allowed to leave. That was the reason why the state of Punjab did not arrest him at the border before he could enter Kashmir.

Mookerjee's death in custody, which Hindu nationalists believe was murder, made Article 370 the hottest issue on the Hindu nationalist agenda. After the formation of the BJP in 1980, in every election manifesto, the party declared its unwavering commitment to abrogate Article 370.

As a BJP functionary, Modi had, while crisscrossing Kashmir for two decades, developed extensive knowledge of the ground reality from the locals. He was a part of the three-member BJP team in August 1992 to study the Kashmir situation. As the BJP's National Secretary in the 1990s, Modi was the election-in-charge of J&K.

Modi realized over the decades that Article 370 had resulted in corruption, separatism and lack of good governance in Kashmir. Significantly, after he was declared the BJP's Prime Minister candidate, Modi addressed a huge election rally in Jammu on 1st December 2013. He extolled Maharaja Hari Singh as a social reformer with foresight.

Narendra Modi's approach to Article 370 was not only due to his ideology of 'India First' but also his commitment to bring good governance to the suffering people of Kashmir. As soon as he became Prime Minister, the Gujarat transformative model was applied to Kashmir.

In his first term (2014–19), Kashmir achieved, amongst other things, 100% Open Defecation Free status, 100% household electrification; road connectivity rose from 45 to 80%; rural roads tripled; collateral-free loans and life insurance increased manifold for the underserved.

Modi was now convinced that Article 370 had to be eliminated for the development of J&K. Of course, in addition, it was a part of the Sangh-BJP agenda for a nationalist India. Modi did exhaustive homework for five years on Article 370 during his first term. Every constitutional option was assessed.

The abrogation of Article 370 was not at all a simple affair and was fraught with multiple constitutional complexities. Most experts in the country, including ministers in the BJP, thought that achieving this was legally complicated. Modi had, however, mastered a plan in 2014. He was clear that this plan required huge work and would only be implemented during his second term in office.

Following the Pulwama attack on 14th February 2019 (when a Pakistan-sponsored suicide bomber rammed an explosive-laden vehicle into a convoy carrying Indian soldiers, killing 44 Indian servicemen), and the retaliatory Balakot air strike by India on the terrorist group in Pakistan, which had claimed credit for the attack, the national sentiment was firmly behind the BJP. Modi had just won a second term with a larger majority. The political opposition was squirming in discomfort. Amit Shah was the new Home Minister.

Operation 370 had to be executed swiftly and stealthily.

Strategic planning, extraordinary secrecy and great speed was required to prevent possible unrest in Kashmir and a diplomatic backlash, as also a possible last-minute judicial intervention.

On 1st June 2019, Shah, on his first day in office, was informed for the first time by Modi about the various options on the table which had been explored by Modi and a core team of secretaries during the last five years. Modi outlined in detail the extensive work done and the strategies considered over the last five years as also the steps taken. The key challenges were highlighted. So far, not a single leak had occurred and absolute secrecy going forward was paramount. Modi made it clear that these years of diligent hard work would depend upon the accuracy of the planning and action over the next two months.

Modi's instructions to his new Home Minister were crystal clear. Abrogation of Article 370 must pass all three tests—parliamentary scrutiny and approval, acceptance by the public and the inevitable judicial review. The D-day would be in early August. 'Plan, Prepare and Execute' was Modi's motto. Smokescreens and diversions had to be created within the government to ensure that there was absolutely no leak.

In July 2019, the government received credible intelligence about serious terror threats to the pilgrims in the Amarnath Yatra. Pulwama was fresh in the public mind, where the terrorists had shown hitherto unbelievable audacity by killing Indian soldiers. As a response to this threat, the Government rushed tens of thousands of additional troops to Kashmir.

Sunday, 4th August 2019, was like any other public

holiday in Kashmir. The presence of the troops, though had created an undercurrent of tension. However, all was otherwise peaceful. That Sunday night, Kashmiris suddenly found their mobile phones, landlines, and internet had stopped working. The administration detained all leading Kashmiri politicians, including former Chief Ministers Mehbooba Mufti and Omar Abdullah, and, for good measure, some BJP allies too. Curfew was imposed throughout Kashmir, and there was a media blackout.

Article 370 was born under the wrong stars. To unravel the legal minefield was a huge challenge. Stripped of legalese, the Article itself provided that it could be made 'inoperative', if recommended to the President of India, by the Constituent Assembly of the State of Jammu and Kashmir, which body had been dissolved as early as 1957. Thus, the extinguishing power under Article 370(3) was vested in the President of India. The question, however, was as to who was to recommend the same to the President. Team Modi then hit upon a brilliant constitutional solution, after discarding several other options to achieve the same result.

On 5th and 6th August 2019, the President of India, issued two Constitutional Orders (CO), 272 and 273, first amending Article 367 to substitute the expression 'Constituent Assembly of J&K' with "Legislative Assembly of J&K". At that moment, J&K was under President's Rule and there was no J&K Legislative Assembly, and therefore, under the Constitution, the Parliament of India was empowered to exercise the powers of the J&K Legislative Assembly. The second CO nullified Article 370, as provided in Article 370

(3) itself, like a poison pill, and applied all provisions of the Indian Constitution to J&K.

The Home Minister introduced a legislation in Parliament, splitting the state into two Union Territories, that is, Jammu and Kashmir and Ladakh. The plan was to push through the legislation on the same day in the Rajya Sabha (Upper House of Parliament) where the BJP still did not have a majority. Failure was simply non-negotiable. Ultimately, the Rajya Sabha comfortably passed it on the same day with support from non-NDA parties, including Naveen Patnaik's Biju Janata Dal, BSP, AAP, TDP and the Tamil AIADMK, and a handful of independents.

The next day, on August 6th, in the Lok Sabha, where the BJP enjoyed a clear majority, the Bill passed like a hot knife through butter. The government secured a 2/3 majority in both the Houses. Late that night, Ram Nath Kovind, President of India, signed the final notification. Dr Syama Prasad Mookerjee had been avenged. Narendra Modi had discharged the promise his party had made 68 years ago to the people of India. Article 370 was now history.

New Delhi skillfully managed to control the national and global narrative. Despite a legal minefield of complexities, Operation 370 was executed without a blemish. Modi had performed a modern-day miracle. What was considered as impossible, across the political spectrum, for seven long decades, had become possible due to Modi's near solo efforts for five years (2014-2019).

The expected backlash was relatively muted. Barring sporadic acts of violence, there was no local uprising in

Kashmir. Not a single life was lost. Pakistan was furious. It downgraded diplomatic ties, expelled the Indian Ambassador from Islamabad, and unsuccessfully tried to involve the UN Security Council. The Pakistani Army said that 'it will do everything and anything' to support the Kashmiris. Apart from rhetoric, there was no military action. The Western democracies agreed that it was an internal matter of India and expressed passing concern about the communication lockdown and potential human rights violations.

However, the usual suspects, a section of the Indian intellectual elite and some constitutional experts were aghast. They termed Operation 370 as a 'Constitutional coup', 'a dangerous precedent for democracy', 'a legal sleight of hand', a 'hideous act of colonial annexation and Central authoritarianism' and an act 'eroding federalism'.

Except for the perennially virulent Arundhati Roy, a Booker prize-winning author, and late Abdul Ghafoor Noorani, a respected constitutional lawyer, none of these critics had the guts to say what was uppermost in their mind that the Kashmiri people should have a right of self-determination, and in the meanwhile, the special constitutional status must continue. Saying so would have been political suicide, apart from being exposed to prosecution under sedition and anti-terrorist laws. So, these critics criticized only the manner in which Article 370 was abrogated and the media blackout. These same intellectuals freeze into silence whenever there is a terrorist attack in Kashmir and utter not a word of condemnation or outrage.

Apart from the Congress, which continued to maintain that Article 370 and J&K's special status must continue, most major political parties supported the action. Modi's approval rating soared to its highest, and then came the inevitable judicial challenge in the Supreme Court of India that the abrogation was constitutionally and legally invalid.

Before the Supreme Court, it was contended that the abrogation was illegal and unconstitutional because there was no consent from J&K's elected representatives; it undermined the principles of a Federation and set a dangerous precedent; the detention and media blackout was undemocratic and unconstitutional.

The Government of India, in a sizzling affidavit, placed on record what exactly had transpired in 1947-48, including Patel's explosive letters castigating Nehru. Many legal pundits still apprehended that the Supreme Court may strike down the abrogation as unconstitutional.

On 11th December 2023, a five-member bench of the Supreme Court of India, headed by Chief Justice Dhananjay Chandrachud, unanimously held that Article 370 was temporary and transitory. All the actions taken by the President of India and the Indian Parliament, including the nullification of 370, were legal and constitutional, and the Supreme Court cannot, and would not, interfere with the Parliament's policy decisions. Any resurrection of the infamous Article thus became impossible. Even the government's sworn opponents and critics whispered in private that Operation 370 could not have been achieved without a single leak, by anyone other than Narendra Modi.

In October 2024, assembly elections in Kashmir were peacefully held with a voter turnout as much as 64% despite boycott calls by separatists. Sheikh Abdullah's grandson's regional party won 42 seats and formed the government. BJP was a good second with 29 seats.

Modi would be the first to admit that without divine grace, it would have been near impossible to complete this massively complex constitutional exercise involving the various government departments, the Army, legal experts, management of domestic and international narrative, co-ordination with political allies, without a single leak and without a single hiccup, in hardly 48 hours.

▪

Within 17 weeks of the demise of Article 370, Narendra Modi succeeded in taking yet another long-promised step on the nationalist agenda.

Sections 295 to 298 of the Pakistan Penal Code are the most dreaded and draconian provisions in the world, popularly known as the Blasphemy laws. They are aimed at religious minorities in Pakistan, mainly Hindus and Christians. These laws provide for criminal penalties of rigorous imprisonment up to ten years, as well as life imprisonment, and in one case, a mandatory death penalty. Lynching by mobs of the accused before trial is commonplace, and acquittals are rare. The police and the courts watch helplessly as these laws are often used for settling scores.

Asia Bibi, a Christian farm worker, accused of blasphemy, had to spend eight years on death row before acquittal by Pakistan's Supreme Court, whose judges faced death threats, as clerics brayed for her blood. Under international pressure for her acquittal, she had to flee overnight to Canada and was granted asylum. The Governor of Punjab, Salman Taseer, a progressive leader opposed to the Blasphemy laws, defended Asia Bibi and was shot dead by his own bodyguard. In 2011, Shahbaz Bhatti, a federal minister for minorities and a Christian, called for reform of the Blasphemy laws and was assassinated by unknown assailants. In Lahore in 2013, Joseph Colony, a Christian neighbourhood was burnt to ashes by an enraged mob alleging blasphemy.

Pakistani judges are reluctant to dismiss cases due to threats to their families. Despite severe international condemnation of these laws, including by the United Nations, the European Union and various human rights groups, no reform has been possible due to violent protests from Islamic groups like Tehreek-e-Labbaik, Pakistan. Christians and Hindus, almost all of Indian origin, were disproportionately affected.

The story of Bangladesh, now another Islamic State, which was slightly better than Pakistan, is getting worse after the recent coup, which ousted Sheikh Hasina from power. Nearly 8% of its population is Hindu. Attacks on Hindu temples, homes and businesses are rising. Abhijit Roy, a Hindu blogger, was killed by extremists for raising these issues.

Afghanistan, under the Taliban, though a bit mellowed recently, was not a happy place for religious and ethnic minorities. International agencies had identified Sikhs, Hindus, Christians and Jews as most at risk. Many migrated to India or other countries. In March 2020, an ISIS gunman attacked a Sikh Gurudwara in Kabul, killing 25 people.

Taliban decrees non-Islamic worship to be punishable by death or imprisonment.

The BJP, in its 2019 manifesto, promised to enact legislation to amend the citizenship laws of India to provide protection and citizenship to religious minorities from these three neighbouring countries, who faced persecution. This was in keeping with the philosophy of the Sangh and the BJP about assimilating persecuted Indians as citizens of India. The country is morally obliged to provide shelter and refuge to Hindus and other minorities of Indian origin anywhere in the world.

The legislation sought to amend the Citizenship Act to provide Indian citizenship to six religious minorities in Pakistan, Bangladesh or Afghanistan—Hindus, Sikhs, Buddhists, Jains, Parsis and Christians—who had entered India before 31st December 2014, the cut-off date, and were continuously residing for more than five years, the minimum period, provided they were earlier residents or citizens of these three countries.

In the same electrifying manner as Article 370, on December 9, 2019, the Lok Sabha passed the Citizenship Amendment Bill with 311 votes in favour and 80 against. The Rajya Sabha passed the Bill two days later, which received Presidential assent and became law on 12th December 2019.

The religious minorities covered by this legislation excluded Muslims. While the legislation does not affect any Indian Muslim citizen, it excludes Muslims from those three countries from obtaining citizenship under the CAA. There was logic in Amit Shah's assertion that Muslims were not included in this legislation, as they were 'majority and not minorities in Pakistan, Bangladesh and Afghanistan', and obviously, therefore, not a persecuted religious minority. Apart from this legislation, India legally grants asylum to anyone who qualifies, including Muslims.

India was not the first democracy to introduce such legislation. As early as July 1950, Israel passed the Law of Return, granting Jews anywhere in the world the right to immigrate to Israel and become citizens on the basis that Israel is the homeland for all Jewish people. Anyone born to a Jewish mother or converted to Judaism, provided he is not a member of another religion, is included within its purview.

As was expected, the Congress and a section of the elite vehemently opposed the legislation because it violated the fundamental right of equality before the law by excluding Muslims. More than 140 petitions challenging the legislation are pending before the Supreme Court. Also, on the ground that it violates a basic feature of the Constitution, namely, secularism, their favourite bugbear.

The Supreme Court refused to stay the implementation of the Act, and the same has therefore already been implemented. On humanitarian grounds, the legislation appears unassailable. It is undisputed that Muslims are in a majority in those three countries and, therefore, their exclusion from the ambit of the CAA is a logical corollary.

India is fulfilling its civilizational duties to provide shelter to persecuted Indic communities in Islamic theocracies like Pakistan, Bangladesh and Afghanistan, who were 'left behind' at the time of the Partition. India, as a refuge, for those who were intending to stay in India but had involuntarily ended up in a hostile theocratic environment.

The third item on the nationalist agenda was the construction of the Ram temple at Ayodhya.

CHAPTER SEVEN

The Return of Ram

ZAHIR-UD-DIN MUHAMMED BABUR, born in present-day Uzbekistan, with 12,000 soldiers and a clever use of gunpowder and artillery, defeated and killed Ibrahim Lodi, who had 100,000 soldiers and 1000 war elephants, in the Battle of Panipat, on 21 April 1526, and founded the Mughal Empire, which would rule large parts of India for over 300 years. Immediately after the battle, Babur constructed a mosque at Panipat to commemorate his victory.

Babur had warfare in his genes. On the paternal side, he was a descendant of Timur the Lame, who in 1398, had massacred a hundred thousand captives in Delhi on a single day; and on the maternal side, a descendant of Genghis Khan, who during his carnage career in Asia, Persia and Europe, is recorded to have killed between 20 to 40 million people. However, there is nothing to suggest that Babur emulated his genocidal ancestors in India.

It was commonplace for Islamic invaders to quickly construct mosques in countries that they had conquered and occupied, to signal that Islamic governance had been established.

From his autobiography, *Baburnama*, it appears that Babur did not much like 'Hindustan' and yearned for his native Samarkand. Before he could return, he died at Agra, 47 years old, and was buried in Kabul. During the short stay of four years in India, Babur asserted Mughal rule over the Gangetic plain.

He sent the General of his army, Mir Baqi Tashkendi, to Oudh or Awadh, that is, Ayodhya. One of Mir's first tasks was to construct a mosque to symbolize the new ruler who had vanquished the Delhi Sultanate of Lodi. Apart from Panipat, Babur had constructed mosques in Kheragarh and Sambhal in Uttar Pradesh. Mir constructed the mosque in Ayodhya, which was grand (three onion-shaped domes and a vast courtyard) and, most importantly, situated at a spot that dominated the skyline of Ayodhya.

Across religions, it has been a practice to build temples, mosques, cathedrals and shrines on elevated ground, such as hills and mountains, or raised platforms, which dominate the skyline. Height symbolized spiritual proximity to the divine. Religious structures on high ground also convey sovereignty and territorial control. A prominent skyline enhances the spiritual aura of the structure. The devotee must be made to realize how small he was before God. Hence, selecting the right spot was crucial.

Ramkot, in the centre of Ayodhya, is where all devout Hindus believe that Lord Ram was born. Every Ramnavami, devotees converge from all over. On an elevated platform or mound, sanctified over the centuries, there stood an ancient temple, which dominated Ayodhya's skyline.

Although there is no evidence to suggest that Babur was an iconoclast like his direct lineal descendant, Aurangzeb, who destroyed Hindu temples at Kashi Vishwanath and Mathura, Mir nevertheless represented Babur, a victorious conqueror, who obviously saw the existing temple as a mere obstruction in his path.

It is undisputed, and now established by archaeological evidence accepted by the Supreme Court, that there was indeed a pre-existing religious structure or temple precisely on the spot where Mir constructed the Babri Masjid, whose stone pillars bore Hindu motifs or carvings, further evidence that it was repurposed from the debris of the structure of the earlier temple.

Senior Counsel, Rajeev Dhavan, appearing for the Muslim parties, admitted before the Supreme Court that 'we are not disputing that there could have been a Buddhist structure or a temple underneath the mosque.' The Archaeological Survey of India reported to the Court that the evidence unearthed suggested a large pre-Islamic structure beneath the Babri Masjid, which had elements consistent with Hindu religious architecture.

Neither Babur nor Mir could have ever contemplated the horrendous consequences, the construction of this mosque would entail for the people of India, some 450 years later.

Soon after the British quelled The First War of Indian Independence in 1857, they imprisoned the last Mughal emperor, the poetic Bahadur Shah Zafar in Rangoon, signalling the end of the Mughal Empire, riots broke out at the Babri site which led to the construction of a brick wall or the famous Ram Chabutra, in the outer courtyard, where Hindus once again began to worship Ram. Hence, the collective wishes of the Hindus, for worshipping Ram at the site, spontaneously manifested as early as 1858.

Nearly a hundred and thirty-four years of sporadic litigation followed (1885-2019). A few months before Narendra Modi was born, in December 1949, an idol of Ram appeared overnight in the sanctum of the Babri Masjid, which led to a law-and-order situation, and ultimately, the halting of Muslim prayers. Over the years, skirmishes and court cases proliferated.

The VHP had been consistently demanding the construction of the Ram temple on the site. Then in a strange twist of events, Prime Minister Rajiv Gandhi of the Congress, reeling under the aftermath of the Bofors scandal, and widely accused of appeasing the Muslims over his overruling of the Supreme Court judgement in the Shah Bano maintenance case, panicked, and did a balancing act to appease Hindus, by allowing the Vishwa Hindu Parishad to lay a foundation stone for the Ram temple at the site; and the doors of the Masjid were unlocked for Hindu worship by a local Court under pressure. Rajiv ended up appeasing neither community.

The first chanting, which Narendra Modi heard as a child, was his mother continuously repeating Sitaram, which uplifted her spirits and energized her during the heavy day-long toil. From the tales of Ramayana, which his mother narrated to him and his siblings, he was greatly impressed by the ultimate sacrifice of Ram, despite his unfair banishment and exile for 14 years. This is how God functions when he walks as a man, she often used to say. Ram, as *Maryada Purushottam*—the ideal man who functions within the limits of dharma—became embedded in Narendra's consciousness. As the just King who acted without fear or favour, Ram came to occupy a sacred place in Narendra's heart and mind.

During his sojourn in North India and the Himalayas, Narendra visited the Ram Chabutra at Ramkot and learnt from a priest about the Babri Masjid. A mosque erected by a foreign conqueror after razing to the ground an ancient temple was difficult for young Narendra to digest.

How come his history textbooks during school did not have a whisper about this, wondered Narendra. Akbar had founded a world religion; the devout Humayun had sacrificed his life for his son Jehangir; Shahjahan constructed the ethereal Taj Mahal; Aurangzeb was so pious and simple, even though he possessed of great wealth. This was all that his textbooks said. As if India was thanking these great benefactors for having taken the trouble to invade India and rule it. Why does our history gloss over these invaders? he had asked his mentor in the Sangh. He was told that according to the Nehruvian world view, it was better to sterilize and whitewash history than risk inflaming communal passions.

Later, Modi would read history written by eminent Indian historians, most of them Marxists, referred to as the 'Cambridge-Aligarh school', who with a straight face state that these invaders of Islamic origin came to India, not really with the primary objective of iconoclasm or destroying temples, but only to plunder its wealth.

Jawaharlal Nehru was not too far behind. In a letter dated June 1, 1932, he wrote to his daughter Indira, about Mohammed Ghazni, who invaded India 17 times, and in 1025 CE, broke the most sacred jyotirlinga in the Somnath Temple, as follows: 'Muhammad of Ghazni was hardly a religious man. He was a Mohammedan, of course, but that was by the way. Above everything, he was a soldier, and a brilliant soldier. He came to India to conquer and loot, as soldiers unfortunately do, and he would have done so to whatever religion he might have belonged.'[23]

The above was not the only instance. In his Glimpses of World History (1934), Nehru wrote: 'Babur was one of the most cultured and delightful persons one could meet.'

Perhaps, Nehru had not read the following much quoted verse from *Baburnama* where Babur wrote: 'For the sake of Islam, I became a wanderer; I battled infidels and Hindus; I determined becoming a martyr; thank God, I became a Ghazi!'[24]

After Independence, the author and minister, Kanhaiyalal Munshi and Vallabhbhai Patel were instrumental in reconstructing the Somnath Temple. Patel died before

23 Nehru, Jawaharlal, 'Chapter 51: From Harsha to Mahmud in North India', *Glimpses of World History*, Asia Publishing House, New York, 1962, p. 160.

24 Bābur. *The Bābur-nāma in English*. Translated by Annette S. Beveridge, Project Gutenberg, 1922, p. 575. https://tinyurl.com/y82cw8rb. Accessed on 10 September 2025.

the reconstruction was complete. Munshi invited the first President of India, Dr Rajendra Prasad, to inaugurate the temple, which he did, on 11th May 1951, despite great opposition from Jawaharlal Nehru, who directed All India Radio to blackout the President's extremely balanced speech on the occasion.

Negation of history was perhaps more responsible for communal disharmony, noted Modi. Our history textbooks must reflect the true history of the nation; however, uncomfortable it may be.

Modi then learnt in detail about the history of the Babri Masjid and the Ram Janma Bhoomi controversy. Modi was happy to learn that the VHP wanted to bring Ram back to his birthplace.

In 1990, the BJP entrusted Modi to be the principal organizer of the first leg of the Rath Yatra, which Advani was planning from Somnath to Ayodhya. The organizational skills and the attention to the minutest detail of Narendra Modi were evident for the first time on a national scale, when the Gujarat leg of the Rath Yatra succeeded beyond the wildest expectations of its organizers, and even Advani. This was the first involvement of Modi in the Ram Janmabhoomi movement. His participation, though, was limited to the back office and logistics.

Pamulaparthi Venkata Narasimha Rao was a polyglot fluent in more than ten languages; a Sanskrit scholar who translated Hindu scriptures; profoundly seeped into Vedantic philosophy and Hindu rituals; a deeply religious Hindu, who passionately worshipped Ram.

Rao was a veteran Congress minister in Indira Gandhi and Rajiv Gandhi's cabinets, highly regarded for his backroom strategic skills and administrative experience. Rajiv, though, preferred young leaders and did not much care for the old guard in the Congress like Rao, who was progressively marginalized, and had nearly retired from active politics when Rajiv was assassinated in May 1991. Days before the assassination, Rao, with his secretary, was stuck at an airport due to a delayed flight, whereupon the secretary requested the duty manager to open the reserved lounge for Rao. The manager rudely refused, saying it was not possible to accommodate all old former ministers. Days later, 70-year-old PV Narasimha Rao was plucked out of oblivion to become the ninth Prime Minister of India on 21 June 1991. It is not known what happened to the airport duty manager.

In late 1992, Prime Minister Rao received reports from the Intelligence Bureau that there was a serious possibility of the Babri Masjid being demolished. Rao was urged by his office to sack Kalyan Singh, Chief Minister of the BJP government in Uttar Pradesh, and impose President's rule. Also, he was advised to deploy the Army. Rao did nothing.

When the 150,000-strong mob, after a VHP rally, on 6 December 1992, started demolishing the Babri, by clambering all over it, and bringing down all three domes, the Police and the Provincial Armed Constabulary stood by and did not intervene. During this process, Rao was uncontactable and reportedly had locked himself in his bedroom and gone to sleep.

Ramchandra Guha, in his book, *India after Gandhi*,

laments that 'a structure which had seen more than 400 monsoons was reduced to rubble within six hours.'

Post the demolition, communal violence erupted in almost all major cities and towns, in which 2000 perished. Rao, looking disturbed, went on national television and promised to reconstruct the Masjid. The Central government appointed the Liberhan Ayodhya Commission of Enquiry and instructed it to report within three months. The Commission would report, but in June 2009, after 17 years and 48 extensions. The Commission concluded that the demolition was a pre-planned act by Hindu right wing organizations and there had been an institutional failure to prevent the demolition.

Had Rao, a staunch ritualistic Hindu immersed in Sanskrit and Veda, turned a blind eye. The Commission, while exonerating him, did indicate complicity by omission. Some Congressmen accused him of soft Hindutva. Rao and Advani had a lot of mutual respect. As Prime Minister, Rao had kept open back-door channels with Kalyan Singh, the CM of UP. There is reason to believe that the complete inaction on the part of Rao was deliberate.

This is evident from the way a furious Sonia Gandhi, back in power in 2004 when Rao died, refused entry to the hearse carrying his body and the gun carriage, which waited for four hours outside the Congress headquarters on 24, Akbar Road in Delhi. Despite being in power for ten years thereafter, the Congress did not erect a memorial in Delhi for Rao, which was erected in 2015, only when Narendra Modi was Prime Minister. Rao's maternal grandson is today a BJP spokesman.

Decades later, in 2024, the Modi government decided to

posthumously award the Bharat Ratna, India's highest civilian honour, to non-BJP Prime Ministers like Chaudhary Charan Singh and P.V. Narasimha Rao.

The demolition of the Babri was a dilemma for all those who believed in Hindutva, but also the rule of law. Even Advani appeared to be shocked at the turn of events. At the same time, there was no more emotive religious issue for devout Hindus, other than the Ram Janma Bhoomi. The Hindu community had tried to enforce its rights in courts of law for over a hundred years, with no result. The demolition though, was undoubtedly unlawful.

In 1925, in the case of Mullick vs. Mullick, the Privy Council held that an idol of a Hindu deity is a juristic entity. It has a legal personality and can own property, sue and be sued. The Supreme Court reaffirmed in 1999 that a deity in the temple is the legal owner of the temple's property. This is a concept unique to Indian law and jurisprudence.

Thus, litigation was filed by the idol itself, that is, Ram Lalla Virajman, alongside the Niranjan Akhara, versus the Sunni Waqf board. On 30th September 2010, the Allahabad High Court gave its judgement directing a three-way division of the disputed land between the parties, all of whom were extremely dissatisfied and appealed to the Supreme Court, which stayed the Allahabad High Court judgement. Detailed legal arguments were advanced, mediation attempts failed, and periodic hearings in the Supreme Court continued for several years.

In the aftermath of the Godhra riots, despite the victories of the BJP in 2002, 2007 and 2012, Modi, as the

Gujarat CM, consciously decided to focus on development and governance issues, even though every single day, in his morning meditation, Modi promised himself that one day he would personally bring Ram Lalla back to Ayodhya. Though, he never made it through an election issue in any of the three Gujarat assembly elections, which he handsomely won.

The BJP, however, in all its manifestoes in the national elections, consistently promised to construct a grand Ram Mandir at Ayodhya. Post the demolition, the promise remained, but the language was toned down.

Modi had, in his mind, clinically compartmentalized the issue of the Ram Mandir. Gujarat and its chief minister had nothing to do with the construction of the temple. Narendra Modi, at a personal level, and as the Prime Ministerial candidate for the BJP in 2013, was passionately espousing the cause. Therefore, the language of the BJP manifesto for 2014 and 2019 national elections became slightly stronger in stating that the BJP was committed to the construction of the temple within the constitutional framework.

Modi became Prime Minister for a second time on 30th May 2019 with a larger majority than 2014. Article 370 was rendered inoperative and Kashmir no longer had any special constitutional status; the Citizenship Amendment Act became law, and the Constitution Bench of the Supreme Court, after a final mediation attempt failed, completed an unprecedented, continuous day-to-day hearing for 40 days, in the Ram Janmabhoomi case, ending 134 years of litigation. For 27 years after the demolition, both communities had maintained total restraint. All parties to the litigation, and the nation, now tensely awaited the day of judgement.

In the pantheon of Hindu divinities, Ram is the most revered. Krishna, the most loveable and attractive, and Shiva the most worshipped. Ram is unique in being the moral anchor of Hindu civilization. *Valmiki Ramayana* is a civilizational epic, which has been orally transmitted from generation to generation. To millions of Hindus, Ram is a historical figure, not a mythological construct. He was the seventh avatar of Vishnu born in the Treta Yuga around 5000 BCE. Ram is the most prayed- in, personal God and an integral part of the Hindu collective consciousness. By occultists all over the world, Ram, like Moses and Orpheus, is regarded as a Great Initiate. Theosophists regard Ram as a Solar Logos, a God.

Awaiting the judgement of the Supreme Court, Narendra Modi in his capacity as Prime Minister, fervently hoped for an unambiguous verdict, which would put the issue to permanent rest. A unanimous well well-reasoned judgement would ensure acceptance by all the litigants. Modi's prayers were answered when the 5-judge bench pronounced a unanimous, 1045-page judgement, on 9th November 2019.

While the Court held that the demolition of the mosque was deplorable and illegal, the entire 2.77 acres of the disputed land in Ayodhya was awarded to the Hindus for the construction of the Ram temple. Muslims were granted five acres of alternative land at a prominent location in Ayodhya for the construction of a mosque. The government was directed to form a trust within three months to oversee the construction of the temple and allocate alternative land to the Muslims.

The reasoning of the Court was that the archaeological evidence did suggest the existence of a non-Islamic structure beneath the Babri Masjid. Though the Court did not say that Mir had demolished an existing Ram temple. The Hindu belief that the site was the birthplace of Lord Ram was recognized as long-standing and undisputed, while the Muslim claim to have exclusive possession was found to be unproven. Hindus were shown to have consistently worshipped at the site, especially in the outer courtyard and later in the inner sanctum.

Although the judgement is shown to be authored by the controversial Chief Justice Gogoi, it is widely believed that it was actually penned by Justice D. Y. Chandrachud, who later became the Chief Justice of India and was known for his learned, erudite judgements. Interestingly, his father, Chief Justice Y.V. Chandrachud, had given the Shah Bano judgement which had triggered Rajiv Gandhi's decision to allow the VHP to lay the foundation stone for the temple.

Stripped of legalese, Ram Lalla had won hands down. It is not without significance that a 450-year-old issue had been resolved under Narendra Modi's leadership.

Modi played a restrained and calibrated role after the Supreme Court judgement, which ensured that communal harmony was maintained. The Prime Minister solemnly addressed the nation after the verdict and stressed that it was a moment of peace, unity and amity for the country. No major VHP, BJP or RSS celebrations were allowed or encouraged. Modi ensured that all concerned avoided the slightest hint of Hindu triumphalism, and temple campaigners were strictly directed to display silence and humility. Massive security arrangements across the country ensured that not a single incident of any serious violence occurred. Social media was monitored, and provocative content was quickly taken down. This was in no small measure due to Narendra Modi's personality. No exuberant Hindu dared to cross the line in the sand drawn by Modi.

The sagacity and statesmanship of Modi was in full display after the Supreme Court verdict. The Ram Janmabhoomi trust was quickly formed, and on August 5, 2020, significantly the anniversary of the abrogation of Article 370, Narendra Modi laid the foundation stone of the Ram Temple on the precise spot where the temple had existed. In January 2024, Modi inaugurated a nearly complete Ram temple in a nationally televised ceremony.

Before doing so, Modi took an *anushthan* for the successful completion of the Ram temple. For more than eleven days, Modi slept on the ground without any mattress or pillow. He observed strict fasting with only warm water. For several weeks, he chanted mantras for the removal of obstacles. This was in addition to his daily rigorous sadhana and kriya.

Before the *Pran-Pratishthan* of the temple on 22nd January 2024, Modi undertook an eleven day ritual observance during which he retraced key places along Ram's return journey, after defeating Ravan, from Lanka to Ayodhya. Ram's original route was from Rameshwaram to Hampi to Chitrakoot to Prayag.

Modi first performed rituals at Panchavati in Nasik. Then

he travelled to Lepakshi in Andhra Pradesh and worshipped at the famed Kerala temples of Guruvayur and Ramaswamy. In Tamil Nadu, he worshipped at Sri Ranganatha Swamy temple and listened to the Kamba Ramayana recitation. He took holy dips in Rameswaram and went through Dhanushkodi, and thereby he symbolically weaved major South Indian Ramayanic sites.

An emotionally charged Narendra Modi in his address at the *Pran-Pratishtha* of Ram Lalla, on 22nd January 2024, said: 'Our Ram Lalla will no longer reside in a tent. Our Ram Lalla will now reside in this divine temple.'

A visibly moved Modi further mentioned that: 'I am having a divine experience at this moment with whose blessings this great work has been accomplished. Those divine souls, those celestial manifestations, are also present around us at this time. I express my gratitude to all these divine consciousnesses.'

'Lord Ram is connected to every particle of the soul of Bharat', Modi concluded.

While Ram and the displacement from his birthplace were deeply embedded in Narendra's consciousness from youth, circumstances and events occurred, which almost deliberately kept him out of a central role in the Ram Janma Bhoomi movement until he became the Prime Minister.

In 2013-14, when the Congress was desperately trying to embroil him in legal proceedings, had Modi been present at Ayodhya on the day Babri was demolished, and indicted, like other BJP leaders, by the Liberhan Commission, the scales could have probably tipped in favour of the aggressive leaders of the Congress demanding his disqualification, which was being resisted by more balanced leaders like Dr Manmohan Singh, Pranab Mukherjee and Sharad Pawar.

Modi's mission has always been under some kind of spiritual protection. The timing and the nature of the Supreme Court judgement reinforces this belief. As if destiny had decreed that the temple would be inaugurated and constructed, after more than four centuries, only when Narendra Modi was in full command.

Modi's joy knew no bounds. His Ram had returned, after nearly half a Millennium, to His birthplace.

CHAPTER EIGHT

Minority Dharma

MYTHS DISTORT REALITY. They proliferate when reality is sterilized. Myths about minorities create mindsets and stereotypes. Myths are disruptive of peaceful coexistence and can tear apart the fabric of a nation. Myths, therefore, need to be busted.

According to the 2011 census, officially classified six Indian minorities-Muslims, Christians, Sikhs, Jains, Buddhists and Parsis-constituted 19.3% of the population, estimated to have slightly increased to 19.5/20% in 2024. Due to millions of Muslims migrating to Pakistan upon Partition in 1947, the percentage of the Muslim population dipped to 9.8%, and thereafter steadily rose to 14.2%, according to the 2011 census, and is estimated to have remained near constant. Christians, the second largest minority, constitute 2.3%.

In the aftermath of the horrors of the Partition, doomsday predictions made by the likes of Jinnah and Winston Churchill that India would Balkanize and fall apart as a nation proved to be unfounded. Peaceful coexistence and multi-religious living between Hindus and Muslims have been the norm. However, in the post-Partition period of 1947 to 2014, twenty-five major riots happened with an estimated loss of 15,000 to 20,000 lives over 67 years.

After Narendra Modi became prime minister in May 2014, there has not been a single major communal disturbance or riot, barring a solitary episode in a part of New Delhi, in 2020, when 53 persons died in a sudden flare-up arising out of anti-CAA protests.

Modi has always believed that economic prosperity is the biggest enemy of fanaticism and has successfully weaponized development as a tool to eliminate communal violence, both as Chief Minister of Gujarat for 13 years and Prime Minister of India thereafter for another 11 years up to now.

Those calling themselves 'anguished pluralists' like Ramchandra Guha, while grudgingly acknowledging that Narendra Modi is a more popular Prime Minister than Indira Gandhi and as much as Jawaharlal Nehru, characterize him as 'abrasive, angular, polarizing' without substantiating any of these adjectives. Then their intellectual dishonesty reaches a climax when they toss their pet phrase-his controversial past, meaning the Godhra riots 23 years ago. This is near 'Goebbelsian' manipulation of the unsuspecting reader who is not at all informed that multiple independent judicial enquiry commissions, a SIT, and the Supreme Court, have all concluded that Modi was in no manner complicit or even negligent in handling the sudden riots, which broke out in the very first 20 weeks of his ever holding a public office, and that the same were provoked by a premeditated and clinically executed attack.

Another serial detractor, the BBC, bristling with left-leaning agnostic journalists having a visceral dislike of Modi and his popularity, furthers its pet theme of Muslim victimhood and Hindu majoritarianism by releasing, usually near election time, rehashed footage of communal disturbances interspersed with archival footage and selective extracts from Western diplomatic cables. The BBC perhaps perceives Narendra Modi, a nationalist leader, with a demigod-like adoration, as an unhealthy trend.

The Indian income tax surveyed the BBC's offices in Delhi and Mumbai in February 2023. Post the so-called BBC tax 'survey'—a euphemism for a tax raid- the Indian tax authorities accused the BBC of under-reporting of income, mishandling of transfer pricing, and non-compliance with the provisions relating to tax deducted at source for UK-based secondees. Initially dismissed by the BBC as political retaliation by the Indian government, the BBC, after prolonged regulatory and tax scrutiny, restructured its Indian presence by four senior Indian employees of the BBC forming a new Indian entity called 'Collective Newsroom Private Limited', legally distinct from the BBC's UK operations and designed to comply with Indian foreign ownership rules in the media sector. A story in the *Financial Times*, London, in April 2024 confirmed the above position.

While motivated critics make no political impact, they feed myths in the minds of both the Muslim minority and the Hindu majority. By perpetuating these myths, they are doing a singular disservice to the very cause that they claim to passionately espouse. On the other hand, Narendra Modi's popularity among Indian Muslims and Indian Christians is steadily on the rise.

Muslims have begun to clearly distinguish between Modi's development mantra and the BJP, on the one hand, and the hardcore Hindu, on the other. Similarly, they have started to make a distinction between legitimate Hindu nationalism and rabid anti- Muslim communalism. Unlike the Western media and the biased elite, Muslims are accepting of a prime minister who is a Hindu nationalist and a devout Hindu, so long as he is fair and even-handed in ensuring that there is no discrimination against them in socio-economic matters like housing, education and welfare benefits. Most Muslims do not find it offensive or jarring if their prime minister inaugurates the Ram temple at Ayodhya or dips in the Mahakumbh. He has every right as a citizen to practice and propagate his own religion.

An increasing number of Indian Muslims, particularly women, admire and adore Narendra Modi. If India had a presidential system of government like the USA, in a one-to-one contest, Modi is likely to secure substantial Muslim votes. The common Indian Muslim of 2025 is now convinced that Modi may certainly be an ardent Hindu nationalist, but he is, by no means, a communalist or anti-Muslim.

Narendra Modi's compassion for his countrymen has never been selective. In his youth, he expressed his fervent desire to serve India, not only Hindus. As Chief Minister and Prime Minister, each measure for the economically weaker sections that he implemented has equally benefited all communities. No measure or scheme of his government has ever been structured to predominantly benefit Hindus. Zubeda in Saharanpur receives the same benefits that her similarly placed neighbour, Radha, receives. None can deny that the Welfare State in India is religion-neutral.

Gradually and imperceptibly, the thinking of the Indian Muslims is therefore changing. They are getting increasingly disillusioned with fanatic religious preachers, who, they feel, have done nothing to better his life except to propagate hatred. While Narendra Modi has most certainly bettered their life. Rupee for rupee, cooking gas cylinder for cooking gas cylinder, monthly deposit of money directly into their account to monthly deposit of money directly into the account of their Hindu neighbours, there is zero difference. Modi has brought socioeconomic welfare to her doorstep by eliminating financial intermediaries through rapid digitalization. The Muslims feel that they have economically gained substantially under Modi's rule. Time, therefore, to switch loyalties from Maulvi to Modi.

This is reflected in the slow, but steady rise in BJP's vote share of Muslims and Christians. In May 2025, in the local government elections in Assam, the vote share of NDA (of which BJP is the major partner) rose from 5% to 35% in Muslim majority constituencies; even more significantly, 60 to 70% of Muslim women voted for the NDA, resulting in victory even in some 90% Muslim populated constituencies. In February 2025, when the BJP decisively won the Delhi assembly elections, it secured its largest ever Muslim vote share. A similar trend is discernible in Kerala, where Indian Christians have been voting in much larger numbers for the

BJP. This rising trend persists, although, the BJP did not field a single Muslim candidate for the Lok Sabha elections in 2014 and 2019, and only a single candidate in 2024, who lost.

Despite the communal riots in Gujarat in 2002, followed by the most concerted vilification campaign against any leader in the history of independent India, in the assembly elections held in December 2012, the BJP under Modi's leadership secured substantial Muslim votes. No better proof that Muslims were convinced that Modi not only did his best to minimize loss of life but also rehabilitated and made even the traumatized Gujarat Muslims feel secure again. Younger Muslims have begun to prioritize economic growth above identity politics.

Modi's *shakti upasana* is not limited to spiritual matters. Empowerment of women and gender justice has been implemented in the form of a slew of measures, which have been extensively documented. However, his special concern for protecting the interests of Muslim women needs to be highlighted as an integral part of the Minority Dharma.

After the Supreme Court held the practice of triple *talaq* (Muslim husband instantly divorcing his wife by merely uttering the word *talaq* thrice even at a single sitting) to be unconstitutional in 2017 in a petition filed by Shayara Bano, a Muslim wife; in 2019, the Modi government decided to give teeth to this judgement and had a legislation passed which made triple talaq a criminal offence. Although this law resulted in the unfair practice becoming extremely rare and was warmly greeted by women's rights organisations, including delighted Muslim women, the Congress opposed it, saying the BJP's idea was to 'jail Muslim men'. At times, one wonders whether the Congress leaders who make these ludicrous statements are trying to surreptitiously help the BJP.

In the national elections in 2019, and more so in 2022 UP assembly elections, particularly in Western UP, Muslim women voted in large numbers, telling pollsters that they were voting for 'Narendra Modi who had upheld their dignity'. So far though, their regard, respect and affection appear to have remained restricted to Modi.

This is also reflected in the warmest of receptions, which Modi receives, in Islamic countries like Saudi Arabia, the UAE, Indonesia, Malaysia and Nigeria, whose leaders have developed the highest quality of rapport with him, and who genuinely believe that the Indian Muslim is safe under his rule.

Modi's ultimate personal aspiration is not satisfied with merely achieving peaceful coexistence. He wants to change the mindset of the mainstream of both communities. Extremists on either side are altogether a different matter. Attempting to change them alienates them further. However, Modi's task to change mainstream mindsets is also not easy.

After Partition, economically well-off Muslim families migrated to Pakistan, leading to a loss of elite economic presence in India. From 1970 to the beginning of the present Millennium in 2000, NSSO data showed that 52% of Muslims lived below the poverty line, having a literacy rate of 50%, just 4% reached high school, and only 4 to 5 % held government jobs. Most were self-employed or concentrated in low-productivity work. Their access to credit and finance was limited. In November 2006, the Sachar Committee revealed other structural disparities.

In late 2006, surveys showed that Muslim literacy rose to 59% against the national average of 65%. Muslims continued to be underrepresented in the bureaucracy. The unemployment rate was higher than in other communities, and social and private school infrastructure was lacking in Muslim concentrated villages.

From 2007 to 2014, there was progress, yet the gap remained. Urban poverty rate for Hindus was 19%; for Muslims, 34%. Muslim representation in government jobs rose from 5% to 8.5%. In 2009–10, average monthly per-capita spending for Hindus was Rs. 1,123 and for Muslims it was Rs. 980.

Politically, Muslims were underrepresented in Parliament compared to their population and also experienced labour market discrimination. On the other hand, Kerala Muslims benefited from diaspora remittances and social investments, showing remarkably higher literacy and economic mobility. Up to 2014, Muslims significantly lagged behind the Hindu majority in all measurable indicators: education, income, job security, political representation, and access to finance.

In 2014, when Modi became Prime Minister for the first time, he inherited the above position, which was predominantly under Congress rule, despite Congress practising vote-bank politics.

Muslim male literacy rose to 85%. Overall poverty rates have reduced substantially to 4.86% rural and 4.09% urban.

Some studies suggest even a reversal of the Hindu-Muslim wage gap.

Modi has constantly endeavoured to change the mindset of not only Hindus but also other non-Muslim communities, who frequently perceive Muslims as having extra-territorial loyalty, leading to distrust and social alienation, the key structural causes behind Muslims' socio-economic underperformance in India. It cannot be denied that Muslims face discrimination in private sector employment, housing and social integration, and they are underrepresented in security and sensitive government sectors like intelligence and defence. At times, the Indian Muslim feels apprehensive and saddened about palpably hostile and vitriolic social media posts doubting his patriotism and loyalty to India.

Episodes like the 1993 Bombay blasts, the 2001 attack on the Indian Parliament, and the 2008 Mumbai attacks on five-star hotels and other sites, reinforce collective suspicion against Muslims in public discourse. This unfortunate distrust, based on perceived collective guilt or historical baggage, is economically disastrous. Every time a terrorist episode occurs on Indian soil or there is armed conflict with Pakistan, such distrust and dislike increase, adding to the stress of mainstream Muslims. This has led to a ghetto mentality where Muslims feel safe by living in segregated areas. There are several districts in Uttar Pradesh and Bihar where Muslims are in the majority. Doing so also increases their political and electoral clout.

At the same time, the Indian Muslim considers himself happy to live in democratic India and fortunate that he is not in Pakistan. The findings of the internationally reputed Pew Research Centre found that 89% Muslims feel that they are 'very free' to practice their religion, and 95% are proud to be Indian. Muslims have occupied thrice the highest office in the Republic of India as the President of India and have contributed three Chief justices of the Supreme Court of India, and also served as chief ministers of states. The Indian Muslim knows that this would never ever happen for Hindus in Pakistan which persecutes its minorities under draconian blasphemy laws.

Modi has made several bold moves to publicly demonstrate that India values its Muslim patriots as much as anyone else. During the May 2025 Operation Sindoor (serious hostilities between India and Pakistan), the media briefings of the Indian Armed Forces by Colonel Sofiya Qureshi, a decorated Muslim woman soldier, impressed the world.

At a personal level, Modi has always had a warm personal connection with the Muslim community. When his school friend, Abbas, lost his father, he stayed in Narendra's house until he completed his studies. 'My mother, extremely large-hearted, was as affectionate and caring towards Abbas just like she did for all of us siblings,' Modi has recorded in a blog in 2022. The Prime Minister informally consults on a regular basis with different Muslim sects to ascertain their views.

Muslim women could travel for Haj only with a male companion (*Mehram*). Unmarried women, widows, and those not having male relatives, were unable to do so. In 2018, the Modi government abolished the rule and permitted Muslim women over 45 years to travel in groups of four or more, without a male guardian. In the very first year of this reform, 1300 Muslim women could go to Haj. In 2024, the number surpassed 4000.

On a personal level, Narendra enjoys the confidence of the Muslim youth, as someone who cares for them beyond politics. During the 2014 election campaign, as Prime Minister candidate, Modi said: 'I would like to see Quran-carrying Muslim youth also use modern technology like computers.' During an event titled 'Islamic Heritage: Promoting Understanding & Moderation', attended by Jordan's King Abdullah II, Modi reiterated this sentiment, saying that he wanted Indian Muslim youth to strike a balance between spiritual grounding and technological prowess.

Modi's fondness for Sufism is well known. At the Opening Ceremony of the All India Ulama & Mashaikh Board in New Delhi on 17th March 2016, a global conference on Sufism, the Prime Minister said: 'For Sufis, service to God meant service to humanity. Sufism, a celebration of diversity and pluralism, is the voice of peace, co-existence, compassion and equality. Sufism helped shape a distinct Islamic heritage in India, which has emerged as one of the most vibrant hubs of Sufism.'

Yet in his attempts to portray Modi as a communalist, Ramachandra Guha refers to one of Modi's speeches upon being elected as PM where he expressed his desire to free India from '*bara sau saal ki ghulami*' meaning 1200 hundred years of slavery, and states that Modi 'sees Muslim rulers as being as alien, and as evil, as the British'.

Firstly, several of the Islamic invaders who invaded or

ruled India like Mohammed Ghazni (17 times invaded India, destroyed temples including Somnath), Mahmud Ghori (massacres in Ajmer), Alauddin Khilji (destroyed temples and oppressed farmers), the mentally unstable Mohammed bin Tughlaq (mass migrations ordered from Delhi to Daulatabad causing thousands of deaths), Feroz Shah Tughlaq (imposed taxes on non-Muslims, destroyed temples and forced conversions), Timur the Lame (massacred 100,000 in Delhi alone on a single day), and Aurangzeb (reimposed taxes on non-Muslims, desecrated and demolished temples in Kashi Vishwanath and Mathura, persecuted Sikhs and Marathas, imprisoned his father and killed all his brothers), were indeed unmitigated evil.

Secondly, Modi has in no manner implied that Indian Muslims are in any way responsible for the sins committed by these foreign invaders. Thirdly, what Modi meant by the phrase was the mindset of slavery which has not been shaken off even after 1200 years.

It is thanks to this mindset that even after Independence, prominent roads in Delhi were still named after oppressive rulers like Aurangzeb. No country in the world, after attaining independence, commemorates the rule of its most cruel foreign oppressors. After Narendra Modi became PM, in 2015, the name of Aurangzeb Road was changed to Dr Abdul Kalam Marg, the patriotic scientist President of India, a Muslim.

In a column in the *Hindustan Times*, on 9th September 2015, Ramachandra Guha wrote that naming a road in Delhi after Chhatrapati Shivaji, whom he called a regional or feudal ruler, was 'a gross misrepresentation of history', a majoritarian symbolism which eroded secular cohesion.[25] Had valiant Shivaji who died in 1680 at the age of fifty, lived longer, he would have possibly brought the Mughal rule in India to an early end. Perhaps Guha would not have been able to enjoy Bahadur Shah Zafar's ghazals.

From the scholarly writings of experts and historians like Richard Eaton and Francis Robinson, as well as genetic studies like The Indian Genome Variation Consortium, approximately 80% to 90% of Indian Muslims are descendants of the local population who converted to Islam over the centuries, primarily from Hindu, Buddhist, and/or tribal backgrounds. Only a small fraction are descendants of foreign settlers such as Arabs, Afghans, etc. Such conversions occurred either forcibly, or to a limited extent, by lower castes and oppressed groups trying to escape caste discrimination; Sufi saints spreading Islam through spiritual teachings as in Kashmir; and a few, for reasons of political, economic, or social mobility.

The ancestors of Indian Muslims suffered as much as the Hindus when these barbaric foreign invaders unleashed their carnage and genocide. Hence, whitewashing history serves no purpose and only proves counterproductive.

The State, the majority and the minority all have to discharge the Minority Dharma. To ensure peaceful coexistence is the primary goal. The major challenge is the

---

25 Guha, Ramachandra. 'The Way Backward and a Way Forward', *Hindustan Times*, 9 September 2015, https://tinyurl.com/2vyafuyr. Accessed on 10 September.

sheer existence of Pakistan, a rogue State and a failed nation, on the doorstep. Pakistan controls its unhappy populace by crying wolf over India and commits overt and covert acts of aggression. These acts, like the train burning in Godhra, are designed to provoke the majority and cause communal disharmony.

Narendra Modi has brought about a huge transformation in the thinking of the average Muslim. After 11 years of Modi, the Muslim is increasingly convinced that Modi will protect him as much as any other Indian citizen. As literacy rates and education levels of Indian Muslims steadily improve, they have begun to clearly see Pakistan as an enemy, not a friend. Modi never loses a single opportunity to highlight the services of patriotic Muslims in the service of the nation, whether as civilians or in the armed forces.

Decisions such as the abrogation of Article 370 or enactment of the Citizenship Amendment Act or the creation of the Ram Mandir, do not in any manner, adversely affect or prejudice the rights and interests of the common Muslim person in India. His fundamental rights are adequately protected under the Constitution of India and enforced by the Supreme Court and the High Courts. Similarly, any move towards a Hindu Rashtra, as a civilizational and cultural entity, and so long as it is not a theocratic State, is not inimical to the interests of the Indian Muslim. As far as the State is concerned, there is no discrimination against him in economic, financial or money matters. It cannot be denied though that he does face social prejudice and discrimination in day-to-day life, however, that does not make him a second-class citizen vis-à-vis the State.

Social prejudice and stereotyping against innocent Muslims, due to increasing incidents of Islamic terrorism (75% of all high fatality terrorist attacks worldwide between 2000-2025 were by Islamic terrorists), is not limited to India but is sadly a worldwide phenomenon.

Hindu intolerance in certain geographies is on the rise like cow vigilantism and lynching which the Supreme Court has termed as 'horrendous acts of mobocracy', and the Court has recommended enactment of anti-lynching laws. Similarly, cases of assault on Hindu-Muslim interfaith married couples ('love jihad') are indeed triggers for communal disharmony. Critics have deplored, what they term, 'political silence' of the rulers, about these deeply upsetting and morally condemnable incidents. At a personal level, such violent intolerance undoubtedly distresses Modi and other mainstream BJP leaders. At a townhall interaction to mark two years of MyGov platform on 6th August 2016, Modi expressed great anger at 'self-styled *gau-rakshaks*' who run shops in the name of cow protection. Modi asked state governments to prepare a detailed dossier of such people.

However, to publicly condemn each such incident has often been found to aggravate the situation further. Mainstream Hindu politicians are compelled to strike a balance between preventing the occurrence of more such incidents and playing into the hands of extremists wanting to capture the mainstream political space.

The Indian Muslim is gradually learning not to be swayed by the propaganda of the radical elements within the community as well as a section of the intellectual elite, domestic and Western, which is desperately fishing for any incident or episode by which they can make Modi, and his government, look biased.

On the other hand, for the Hindu majority to discharge its minority dharma is equally critical. For decades, the Hindu majority has helplessly watched the appeasement policies of successive governments. It has not been able to express or fulfil its legitimate cultural religious aspirations. The painfully long struggle for creating a Ram Mandir is a prime example. For the first time in the history of independent India, a Prime Minister has been able to deliver to the Hindu majority progress towards its cultural aspirations. The Hindu majority is beginning to appreciate the ongoing work of the Modi government in this direction and gradually learning to have patience and not be provoked by radical propaganda.

Barring a micro-minority of extremists, the ordinary Indian Muslim does not have any extra-territorial loyalty, whether to Pakistan or to militant Islam. And there is a world of difference between Indian Muslims and Pakistani Muslims. In its day-to-day interactions with the Muslims, Hindus and other non-Muslim communities have to shed their irrational prejudice, whose instances are highlighted by the Western media to tarnish the moral stature of the Indian State.

No discussion about the minority issue can be complete without reference to the Uniform Civil Code (UCC), designed as a common law uniformly applicable to all citizens of India regarding personal matters, such as marriage, divorce, inheritance and adoption. This is the unfinished item on the nationalist agenda.

A simple legal reform, unfortunately, has been elevated to become a supercharged emotional issue. At the end of the day, the average Muslim is not really concerned about Kashmir's constitutional status or some amendments to the Citizenship laws which in no manner affects him or even the construction of the Ram Mandir; however, mention UCC, and there is agitation.

A young reader may be pardoned for believing that the UCC is a creation of the RSS, BJP and Narendra Modi. The following quotation will make things clear.

'It is not correct to say that religion is in danger. Religion is not in danger. We are dealing with personal law, not with religion. One nation, one law is the ideal we must aim for. A civil code that applies to all citizens will help unify the country.'[26]

The speaker was Dr B. R. Ambedkar, author of the Indian Constitution, during the debates in the Constituent Assembly, strongly advocating the UCC. Ambedkar calmly refuted every argument of the Muslim members of the Assembly who contended that the UCC would infringe their religious freedom. He correctly submitted that civil laws like inheritance, divorce and marriage were a part of social regulations, not core religious practices. It was about to be accepted by the Constituent Assembly but for the vociferous opposition of Nehru, who ultimately ensured that it would

26 *Constituent Assembly Debates*. Vol. 7, 23 Nov. 1948, discussion on Draft Article 35—Uniform Civil Code, pp. 550–551. Lok Sabha Secretariat, Parliament of India, https://tinyurl.com/yfypcbjb. Accessed on 10 September 2025.

remain only an aspirational Directive Principle of State Policy.

Nothing happened for nearly four decades until Rajiv Gandhi legislated to overturn the Shah Bano judgement relating to the rights of a Muslim woman to claim maintenance, in order not to upset the agitated Muslim clergy. This prompted the BJP to take up the UCC issue.

The 1996 BJP election manifesto raised the issue of the UCC (Article 44 of the Constitution states: 'the State shall endeavour to secure for the citizens a uniform Civil Code throughout the territory of India') as a part of its core ideological triad—the other two being Article 370 and the Ram Mandir. A civil codification of—one nation, one culture, one law.

UCC seems like much ado about nothing. Triple talaq has already been abolished and criminalized. Increase in urbanization, education, and economic pressure, have reduced the incidence of polygamy among Indian Muslims to levels that are either comparable to, or sometimes, even lower than other communities. Muslims themselves are fed-up and perplexed with their personal laws of inheritance, which are mathematically complex with multiple permutations and combinations or are unnecessarily convoluted. For instance, a Muslim cannot bequeath his property under a will to his legal heirs; he cannot bequeath more than 1/3 of his total estate under a will to any other person. Then why such hue and cry about the UCC.

The probable answer is that maybe the above individual reforms are indeed acceptable to the Muslims. However, what they perhaps cannot fathom is the intention of a Hindu majority party for its insistence on the UCC. Will this be followed by a cultural invasion about personal matters like religious education, or religious rituals, or even dress codes, is what the average Muslim apprehends. Hence, a campaign to transparently discuss this reform may well make the Indian minorities realize that the change is not only legitimate, but beneficial to them.

▪

And to end the saga of India's minorities on a positive note, even at the risk of being accused of bias.

Fleeing Arab persecution, Parsi Zoroastrians landed in Western Gujarat sometime in the 9th century, as penniless refugees, to save their Holy Fire. They promised the local Hindu ruler that they would assimilate with Indians, like sugar in milk. Numerically minuscule (60,000 in India, 90,000 in the world), they never demanded reservation of jobs or special rights or political representation as a religious micro minority or any financial assistance. They zealously guard their Holy Fire but never proselytized or seek to convert. They adopted Gujarati as their native tongue and followed Hindu traditions of dress, marriage and birth. They culturally assimilated seamlessly. They gave India, the country that sheltered them in their gravest hour, unstinted loyalty and unconditional love.

With 100% literacy, and women being more equal than men, they provided the first woman doctor, the first woman lawyer, and were pioneers in female emancipation. They gave India several large and rich industrial conglomerates—including the Tatas; the country's first Field Marshal, two Chief of Air staff, one Vice Admiral; numerous decorated war heroes; two Chief Justices of the Supreme Court; the country's most eminent doctors, lawyers, judges and constitutional experts; father of India's atomic energy. They bestowed on the nation non-communal charities of staggering proportions. All this from a minority constituting 0.006% of India's population. They did all this quietly, unobtrusively, and with innate humility. They are adored by Hindus, Muslims and Christians. RSS calls them 'loyal patriotic and self-effacing'. Narendra Modi does not tire of giving their example as the model minority.

The above is not to praise the stellar qualities of the Parsis. It is to underscore how magnanimously the Hindus have gracefully made such achievements possible even by the tiniest micro-minority of India.

CHAPTER NINE

Jai Ma Bhawani

IN THE FIRST twenty years of his life, Narendra Modi witnessed three wars. One ended in an ignominious defeat (Sino-India 1962, Nehru), a partial victory (India Pakistan 1965, Shastri) and a glorious victory (Bangladesh Liberation War 1971, Indira). Modi's love affair for the soldiers had begun during the first two wars, serving them free tea and snacks on the train. During and after the Bangladesh War, as a young *pracharak*, Narendra was actively involved in organizing camps for refugees, collection drives and relief work.

His father had thrown cold water on his fervent desire to be admitted to the nearby Sainik School including on the ground that the family had no money to spare. Narendra was not aware that the admission was virtually free. Destiny was diverting him for a larger role.

In February 1999, at Lahore, Vajpayee and Pakistan's Prime Minister Nawaz Sharif, signed the Lahore Declaration. Within weeks, General Pervez Musharraf, who was Chief of Army Staff, without the knowledge of Nawaz Sharif and the civilian government, sent Pakistan Army regulars disguised as *mujahideen* and occupied strategic Indian mountain peaks in Dras, Kargil and the Batalik sectors. This led to a full-scale war, and India recaptured all key positions by July 1999. In the war, hundreds of Pakistani soldiers died, including the elite Northern Light Infantry. Pakistan suffered international condemnation and was diplomatically isolated. Sharif was forced to plead with President Clinton to de-escalate the situation, which led to a ceasefire.

Just three months after the Kargil War, in October 1999, Musharraf, in a coup, ousted Nawaz Sharif and became the military ruler of Pakistan, and ultimately its President. His authoritarian rule ultimately led to a judicial backlash and political opposition, forcing him to resign in August 2008. To avoid impeachment, he sought asylum in London and Dubai. He tried to return to Pakistan in 2013 to make a political comeback but was barred from contesting elections. He was arrested and charged in several cases including the murder of Benazir Bhutto and for high treason. A Special Court sentenced him to death in absentia. Musharraf suffered from a rare and dreaded disease called amyloidosis, resulting in multiple organ failure. Bedridden and in excruciating pain in his final years, he died in Dubai.

In 1999, during the Kargil War, Modi was the BJP National General Secretary and vocally supported the war effort and pleaded for zero tolerance for terrorism and standing firm at whatever cost against Pakistan.

India suffered the worst terrorist outrages during Dr Manmohan Singh's UPA government (2004-2014). 1000

Indians died and 300 injured. There were 25 major attacks *outside* Kashmir, the Northeast and Left-wing Extremism-affected areas. Mumbai bore the brunt of three bombing and shooting attacks, aimed at creating maximum panic. There was absolutely no retaliation from India. India was labelled as a 'soft state'.

▪

When Modi became Prime Minister in 2014, the military establishment of Pakistan became apprehensive. They knew that Narendra Modi was no Manmohan Singh. He was daring and unconventional. After a long time, the BJP enjoyed a majority on its own. The Pakistani Army knew Modi's philosophy of war. If you hurt my people without cause, I will come into your house and kill you. The Code of Hammurabi: An eye for an eye; a hand for a hand; a life for a life. Gone were the days of measured response; India would retaliate forcefully. Modi's fierce nationalist credentials were public, and so was his resolve to abrogate Article 370 and end Kashmir's special constitutional status, which had given a diplomatic fig leaf so far to Pakistan to hide. Modi appointed the formidable strategist and former Intelligence Head, Ajit Doval, as the NSA. In April 2015, the Prime Minister visited France and revived the stuck up Rafale deal as India badly required fighter jets. For the first time, India had a wartime Prime Minister.

On the other hand, Narendra Modi knew that in Pakistan, he was dealing with a highly unstable enemy not motivated by any national, military, diplomatic, political or economic interest. As General Zia put it: 'Bleed India with a thousand cuts.' Zia died in a plane crash, with his top military command, on a very rainy night on August 17, 1988.

Pakistan's animus against India arises out of pure hatred, revenge psychology, and military-religious extremism. Pakistan's logic is simple. If India is no longer the enemy, Pakistan has no rationale to exist. In conventional warfare, Pakistan is no match for India. The repeated military defeats and dismemberment Pakistan has suffered is ample evidence. However, it has nukes.

In mid-May 1998, under the Vajpayee Government, India successfully tested five nuclear devices. There was great and widespread nationwide patriotic pride and rejoicing. Within two weeks, Pakistan exploded a nuclear device. Ramachandra Guha, in his book, records the above developments, and comments thus: 'Two weeks later, this balloon of patriotic pride was punctured and deflated.'[27]

Before the war, which Lord Krishna knew to be inevitable, he nevertheless decided to go to the enemy camp, as a messenger of peace on behalf of the Pandavas, to make an incredible offer of giving up all claims and rights, if Duryodhana agreed to give just five villages to the Pandavas, which of course, Krishna knew Duryodhana would not. Modi decided to emulate Krishna. He invited Nawaz Sharif to his swearing-in ceremony. He also made a few other overtures

---

27 Guha, Ramchandra, 'Chapter 27: A Multi-polar Polity', *India After Gandhi: A History (3rd Edition, Revised and Updated)*, Picador India, Delhi, 2023, pp. 628-651

of goodwill while warning them through back channels that any terrorist attack on Indian soil will result in India entering Pakistan by crossing the LoC and the International Boundary (IB). And the response will be disproportionate.

Pakistan's civil governments, particularly under Nawaz Sharif and Imran Khan, were by and large sensible and wanted peaceful coexistence. We may not love each other but let us not kill each other. However, the real power has always been enjoyed by the military establishment and the deep State and the ISI, which make civilian governments in Pakistan impotent.

Modi had just returned after attending Nawaz Sharif's daughter's wedding ceremony on 25th December 2015. On New Year's Eve 2015, six terrorists from Jaish-e-Mohammed (JeM) entered the Pathankot Air Force Station in Punjab, receiving logistical support from their Pakistani minders, and launched an attack in the early morning of 2nd January 2016. During this encounter, all six terrorists and seven Indian personnel, including an NSG commando, were killed. India provided evidence of Pakistan's army involvement, including telephone calls traced to Bahawalpur, Pakistan, a town which is a family enterprise of the JeM chief, Masood Azhar.

Modi realized that the Pakistani civil government was not fully involved. Modi showed restraint, even allowing Pakistan's investigation team to visit India, though there was no outcome. In May 2019, India succeeded in its decade-long efforts to list Masood Azhar as an international terrorist. In May 2025, during Operation Sindoor, the Bahawalpur camp was destroyed by the Indian Air Force, and ten close relatives of Masood Azhar were killed, as admitted by a distraught Azhar himself. Pathankot had been avenged.

Within months, in September 2016, four more terrorists from the same group, infiltrated into Uri in Jammu and Kashmir, very close to the LoC, and set fire to military camps, firing indiscriminately. More than seventeen Indian soldiers were killed, many of them while sleeping in tents. While all four terrorists were killed, Modi, on the night of 28th and 29th September 2016, directed the Indian Army to cross the LoC and destroy terrorist camps. In a Surgical Strike, more than fifty terrorists were killed.

Modi had signalled a new doctrinal shift from passive deterrence to active and calibrated response. India succeeded in placing Pakistan on the FATF grey list for terror financing. Foreign investments dried up and Pakistan's banking system came under strain.

Modi's first term in office was about to end, and elections were scheduled in May 2019. The inexperienced ex-cricketer, Imran Khan, was Prime Minister of Pakistan. ISI believed that Modi would be preoccupied with the election campaign, as BJP appeared to be facing headwinds of anti-incumbency.

On 14th February 2019, a 22-year-old indoctrinated Kashmiri local, rammed a SUV, on National Highway 44, connecting Jammu and Srinagar, near Lethpora in Pulwama, into a convoy carrying Central Reserve Police Force personnel. Dar was a suicide bomber trained by JeM, and the SUV was packed with 300 kilograms of RDX and ammonium nitrate. 44 CRPF personnel died and many injured. JeM claimed responsibility for the attack.

Although elections had not been formally announced, hectic unofficial campaigning was underway. Modi was on the way to Rudrapur in Uttarakhand to launch a development project, stopping en route at the Jim Corbett National Park for a shooting to promote wildlife conservation and tourism. He cut short the shooting and abandoned the Rudrapur trip, in order to receive continuous briefings from Delhi, despite poor internet connectivity. After reviewing various options, Modi remarked: 'This is not a time for usual response. We need to respond through action.'

In keeping with the new policy of calibrated response, it was decided to target Balakot, the responsible terrorist camp in Pakistan occupied Kashmir (PoK). Knowing that retaliation was certain, Pakistan was on a high alert and its air force, quite professional despite financial constraints, was in scramble readiness. Some in Modi's strategy team advocated a stronger response like attacking Rawalpindi or targeting military bases in Pakistan. Without the slightest hesitation, Modi overruled them. A full-scale war was not, at that stage, in India's interest.

SPICE -2000 bombs from Israel, which had penetrating warheads and bunker-busting capability, each weighing 1000 kgs, was the munition of choice. 300 kgs of explosives have been used in the suicide attack on our Jawans, said Narendra Modi, dump five times the amount of munitions on Balakot.

A crack team of ace IAF pilots were assembled with only the Group Leader knowing about the mission. The enemy had to be outwitted, and subterfuge was used. A 'conceal-reveal' strategy to misguide was adopted.

On 26th February 2019, a select group of twelve Mirages, appearing to be participating in a routine exercise, hopped from one base to another until they landed in a small airbase somewhere in North Kashmir. India had correctly read Pakistan's strategic thinking that this time the Indian retaliation would target military bases in Pakistan and not be limited to strikes in PoK, and that India would most certainly use its larger and more powerful Sukhoi aircraft. On the night of the attack, many Sukhoi aircraft were spotted by the enemy, taking off from somewhere in Rajasthan and appearing to be heading towards Rawalpindi. Pakistan was focused only on the Sukhoi.

The Sukhoi never came. Instead, the tiny Mirages, more capable of avoiding radar than the larger Sukhoi, flew low and whizzed across the LoC, and carried out a successful Air Strike by releasing six Israeli bombs on the Balakot camp killing 300 to 350 terrorists. 6000 kgs of munitions was dropped. These bombs would penetrate deep but not show much visible structural damage which led Pakistan to later claim that the IAF had bombarded some forest land and none had been killed.

The next day, Pakistan symbolically retaliated, and in the ensuing dog fight, Wing Commander Abhinandan, an Indian pilot, bailed out in Pakistan occupied Kashmir (PoK), was beaten by a mob, and captured by Pakistan, who released a video showing him in captivity, in violation of the Geneva Convention on Prisoners of War.

This was a turning point for Modi. India demanded immediate return of the pilot. Any harm to Abhinandan would result in an escalation by India, Pakistan was informed. Mercury was soaring in New Delhi, every passing hour. Western intelligence informed Imran Khan that an enraged Modi may be contemplating attacking Pakistan's nuclear installations. A highly nervous Imran Khan desperately tried to speak to Modi, whose office categorically informed the Pakistani PMO that talks will start only after the release of the pilot. Modi piled on the pressure by personally phoning leaders in Saudi Arabia and UAE to inform that his patience was truly running out. So was Imran Khan's bravado. He made a statement to the Pakistani Parliament that 'in the interest of peace, Pakistan was unconditionally releasing the pilot to India'. Abhinandan became a national hero, was awarded the Vir Chakra and later promoted to Group Captain. 'I am sorry, sir. I am not supposed to tell you that', his statement to his Pakistani captors, became famous as a mark of military restraint. The global community realized for the first time that terror charges against Pakistan will have to be taken seriously.

Wing Commander Abhinandan was not the only hero. Narendra Modi's popularity reached new heights. The electoral sentiment turned overwhelmingly in favour of the BJP, and it won 303 seats in the national elections, its best ever. A resolute and determined Narendra Modi returned as Prime Minister for a second time.

Narendra Modi values his men in uniform above everything else. They warmly reciprocate his love and affection. Donning military gear, Modi regularly visits soldiers at sensitive sites like Kargil and Siachen. He celebrates every Diwali with the armed forces asserting that they are his only family. However, his actions are not symbolic.

Modi initiated several measures for the welfare and dignity of soldiers. One Rank One Pension (OROP) ensures that retired soldiers of the same rank and service length get equal pension regardless of their retirement year. He created the post of Chief of Defence Staff (CDS), a single point military advisor to the government, ensuring synergy and coordination across the three wings of the armed forces. He is constantly endeavouring to restructure the armed forces into Integrated Theatre Commanders for more effective coordination. In 2022, he introduced a scheme of short-term contract soldiers called Agniveers, to serve for only four years, with twenty-five percent of them ultimately retained; with the objective of a youthful force, less pension burden, and inculcating military discipline in civilians. Narendra Modi is clearly a soldier's prime minister.

The Prime Minister supervises each major decision regarding cyber defence infrastructure, space command, and weaponry tests. He plays a major role in military diplomacy with QUAD, France, Russia, USA, and Israel. He personally monitored 100% technology transfer and no-royalty clause to ensure smooth indigenous production of AK–203 assault rifles in India, right upto the establishment of the facility in Amethi. Foreign direct investment ceiling limit in defence was raised from 49 to 74% under the automatic route, and 100% with government approval. In 11 years of Modi, FDI in defence has exceeded Rs. 6,000 crores. In 2015, Modi succeeded in corporatizing 41 ordnance factories in the country which were producing suboptimal defence equipment. Modi was enraged to learn that royalty was being paid without any time or amount limit to the Russian original equipment manufacturer for T-72 tanks, which were then manufactured entirely in India. He personally convinced President Putin that this was unfair, and the practice ended. This is the level of micro detailing and monitoring by Modi in defence matters.

Modi's personal equation with successive US Presidents resulted in the US designating India as a major non-NATO ally and accorded it STA-I status, enabling the transfer of key defence technologies, critical for the national security of India. In the last decade, defence exports by India have increased 34 times, while more than 5000 defence items have been indigenized.

▪

Baisaran valley in Pahalgam, situate at an altitude of 8,000 feet, surrounded by dense pine forests and the snow-clad Pir Panjal mountains, is one of the most scenic places in Kashmir. Not accessible by car from Pahalgam, the muddy road, by trek or pony ride, takes nearly an hour.

In the tranquil afternoon of Tuesday, 22 April 2025, as a gentle breeze blew and children jumped on trampoline and the place was buzzing with tourists riding ponies, the first shots were heard at 1.50 p.m.

Emerging from the thick pine forests, five Pakistan sponsored terrorists, herded the stunned tourists mostly from Uttar Pradesh, Madhya Pradesh and Maharashtra, asking their religion and forcing them to take an Islamic verse test.

25 men were identified as Hindus and shot dead at point blank range, mostly in the head, along with a local Muslim pony operator who tried to intervene. The terrorists told the widows: 'Go and tell your Modi what happened here.' Firing celebratory gunshots, they disappeared into the pine forests. Their celebrations would not last long. Within days, in July 2025, three of them including their leader, Suleiman, were killed by the Indian forces.

For the next fortnight, a War Room was set up under the day-to-day supervision of the Prime Minister, NSA Doval and Lt. General Chauhan, CDS. The Integrated Defence Theatre Commanders, recently created under Modi, swung into action.

PoK is a thin strip of land sandwiched between Pakistan and the Union Territory of Jammu and Kashmir, illegally occupied by Pakistan after the 1947-48 invasion of Kashmir.

The PM, as in each such earlier action, personally studied the images and maps of the twenty-one main terrorist sites operated by Pakistan. None in the War Room would have been surprised had the PM recited by heart for each of the sites, the names, locations, functions and affiliations, and the reasons for their selection.

Nine terrorist camps–four in Pakistan and five in PoK—were identified including Shawai Nalla in Muzaffarabad, where the Pahalgam terrorists had been trained. Muridke, in Pakistan, was where Ajmal Kasab and David Headley had been trained. Kasab had been hanged for killing many civilians in the Mumbai terrorist attack in 2008. Headley alias Dawood was the terrorist mastermind behind those attacks and was sentenced to imprisonment in USA for 35 years.

In the early morning of 7th May 2025, at seven minutes before 1.00 a.m., Indian Air Force Rafale fighter jets took off from a base in North Kashmir, under the guise of a training exercise and employing radar blackouts to maximize surprise. Last ten days, they had done this repeatedly, to make the enemy complacent. They would not cross the LoC or the IB and launch cruise missiles and the precision-guided munition like BrahMos, Crystal Maze-2, Rampage and SCALP missiles, from Indian territory itself.

At 1.05 a.m., Operation Sindoor began. Three IAF Rafale released the munition on site number One, Shawai Nalla—operated by Lashkar-e-Taiba, whose proxy, the Resistance Front (TRF), had initially claimed responsibility for the Pahalgam attack. The missiles killed several terrorists who were sleeping. Later, in July 2025, the Modi government would successfully manage to convince the US State Department to classify TRF as a 'Foreign Terrorist Organisation' and 'Specially Designated Global Terrorist'.

In 23 minutes, before 1.30 a.m., all nine targets were hit. Some repeatedly. About 100 terrorists were killed.

The PM oversaw in the minutest detail a tri-service military operation to target terrorist infrastructure and neutralize their operational capability.

Simultaneously, the PM responded to communications from leaders of countries across the globe, telling them that it was a calibrated response to degrade terrorist infrastructure and show resolve, without a full-scale war.

Three Pakistani Aircraft Hangars at Sukur, Bholari and

Jacobabad (F16) were destroyed including a few F16 in the Hangar. A surface-to-air missile downed a Pakistan's AEW& C aircraft. Missiles landed very close to Pakistan's Army General Headquarters (GHQ) at Chaklala near Rawalpindi. Eight Pakistani airbases were hit. Neutral defence analysts subsequently confirmed that post-strike satellite imagery showed significant structural damage, particularly to Bahawalpur and Muridke camps in Pakistan.

Pakistan may have expected that Indian strikes would be limited to PoK, and not Pakistan, and hence, the surprise. India's signal that it can, at will, hit any place anywhere in Pakistan or PoK which supports terrorist infrastructure.

While it is true that in military campaigns, one cannot count bodies, or loss of hardware like planes, the mindless cycle of terrorist attacks, followed by retaliation and counter-retaliation, resulting in the loss of lives of the armed forces as well as civilians, disturbs Narendra Modi to the core. As the gory attack in Pahalgam demonstrates, after every ten to fifteen years, a jingoistic General comes to power in Pakistan, like Zia or Musharraf or Munir, who detests India and wants to leave a mark as a national hero in Pakistani history.

Days before the Pahalgam attack, Munir, who has a religious fundamentalist background, publicly reiterated Jinnah's two-nation theory stating that Muslims and Hindus, primordial nations, were different in everything and cannot coexist. This was extreme rhetoric from a man who effectively controls Pakistan. Neutral international defence analysts called this 'dog-whistling' the terrorists to attack.

■

In 1960, the Nehru government, without placing it before Parliament, had signed the Indus Waters Treaty (IWT) with Pakistan, described by neutral international experts as 'one of the most one-sided waters sharing pacts in the world'. Pakistan got exclusive control over 80% of the water by volume, that is, the three largest Western Rivers and India over three Eastern Rivers. In the absence of IWT, India as the upstream riparian State could have controlled the flows. The IWT, therefore, became Pakistan's lifeline for 90% of its food production. Further, the IWT imposed design and storage limits on hydropower projects in India. This provision has been repeatedly used by Pakistan in the past to sabotage Indian hydro projects.

The signing of the IWT led to an unprecedented uproar in the Parliament when opposition benches along with some Congress members, criticized Nehru, 'for giving away too much'. Nehru was described as an umpire in a cricket match, (acting like a neutral observer instead of batting for India). Nehru said that he did not understand so much fuss over a few buckets of water. Ayub Khan later relied upon the IWT to try and convince America that 'Pakistan needed some miles across the Chenab to secure its water resources'.

In response to the Pahalgam terror attack in April 2025, in a masterstroke, India put the IWT in abeyance on the ground of a fundamental change in circumstances, that is, terrorism and national security concerns. Article 62 of the Vienna Conventions on Treaties justifies such action. The Home Minister declared that the IWT will never be restored, and water will be diverted to water deficient Indian territories like Rajasthan. In his 2025 Independence Day address, Modi reiterated this new policy: blood and water cannot flow together. India has rejected the jurisdiction of the Permanent Court of International Arbitration over the IWT. India has stopped sharing hydrological data with the enemy and is actively pursuing a hydrological pivot, fast-tracking projects on these rivers to reconfigure the water management in India's favour.

Modi has categorically declared that none will undermine India's water sovereignty. IWT was a World Bank foisted one sided treaty upon a then dependant India, which the Modi government has had the courage to suspend after 65 years. This move is already wreaking nerves in Pakistan as evidenced by Munir's bravado of threatening to destroy India's hydro projects. A pressure point on Pakistan's jugular which will cause incalculable damage to its economy.

Issues can be resolved, not irrational hatred. What makes Pakistan so dangerous not only to India but to world peace, is, that it is a nuclear-armed, near-bankrupt country, which may be about to explode and disintegrate. This is not wishful Indian thinking.

Pakistan is facing an existential crisis as never before. It is not a natural nation, as often wrongly described, but a combination of ethnicities unified by force. Baluchistan, rich in gas and minerals, has several insurgent groups that constantly attack Pakistani assets and forces. The people of Baluchistan complain of genocide-level military operations and torture. Historians call it 'East Pakistan 2.0'. Sectarian violence between Sunni, Shia, and other sects regularly disturbs the peace of cities like Karachi.

Pakistan is tottering on bankruptcy and survives on IMF loans and largesse. The army is at war with popular leaders like Imran Khan who is imprisoned.

Islamic nations like UAE and Saudi Arabia have distanced themselves from Pakistan, which is increasingly isolated. Even Iran and Afghanistan have no sympathy for Pakistan's territorial claims. Its only supporters are China, Turkey and Azerbaijan. The probability, that Pakistan will be balkanized or disintegrate is quite strong.

If Pakistan disintegrates or is dismembered, in the medium term, it may initially prove to be a headache for India. Baluchistan would be inclined to align with Iran. Sindh would be independent. Pashtuns (KP), an area with reserves of the much sought after antimony rare earth mineral, may merge with Afghanistan. Only Punjab would remain as a rump. Terrorist groups like JeM may go berserk and try to capture nuclear facilities. At this stage, India is truly blessed to have Modi as its leader, with all his intuitive sagacity and huge hands-on defence experience.

Many hawks urge that India ought to pursue a long-term strategy to weaken Pakistan internally, for instance, by supporting Baluch freedom fighters. Israel, with American help, has recently caused a setback to Iran's nuclear trajectory. Let Israel use Indian airspace to take out Pakistan's nukes, the hardliners suggest. Rajiv Gandhi too had flirted with the idea of a strike on Pakistan's Kahuta nuclear facility but aborted it under American pressure. Sometimes one does not know which country really controls Pakistan's nukes.

Modi is an oasis of calm, unmoved by any such radical ideas, including from his party, who unaware of all the relevant facts, advocate action that can result in untold carnage. Pakistan is disintegrating on its own anyway. Someone had predicted this in 1947 itself.

Arvind Ghosh, born in Calcutta in 1872, was educated at Cambridge and was to join the prestigious ICS. Instead, he became a revolutionary freedom fighter. After being jailed for a year, Ghosh was acquitted in the Alipore Bomb Case, in 1908. Two years later, he had a profound spiritual awakening and moved to French-controlled Pondicherry, dedicating himself to matters spiritual including India's spiritual destiny. Legend has it that when the British police tried to arrest him, they would see a hundred Arvind Ghosh around them.

Arvind Ghosh was now Sri Aurobindo, India's most outstanding intellectual mystic. His books, *The Life Divine*, and *Savitri*, became world famous. From 1920, till his passing in 1950, he gave darshan only four times a year, as he was deeply immersed in his spiritual sadhana. Thousands of disciples testified that they could only see resplendent light, instead of his face, during the darshan. As early as 1918, he had predicted that India would attain independence within a few decades; significantly, India gained Independence on his birthday.

During his days with the Sangh, Narendra Modi had heard the recording, with great fascination, of a radio broadcast from All India Radio station at Tiruchirapalli made by Sri Aurobindo on 15th August 1947, Independence Day, when the sage spelt out five visionary dreams for India and the world. These were spiritual predictions of what he called 'Supra-mental Vision', and an intuitive higher form of consciousness. He called the Partition as something which would be undone, and India would be reunited; not by military conquest but spiritual-cultural reunification of the Indian sub-continent, as *Akhand Bharat*. Aurobindo predicted the decline of Western imperialism and the rise of Asian nations like India and China. In particular, India as the spiritual heart of the world—the cradle of *Sanatan Dharma*—whose wisdom, yoga, and inner science would help humanity evolve. 'She must rise and fulfil her spiritual destiny', said Aurobindo.

Aurobindo made extremely interesting observations in his broadcast on the Partition and Pakistan. He said that Pakistan was born of a false story, and unity would eventually be restored and returned to the deep civilizational unity of Bharat.

The Sangh and Modi regard Sri Aurobindo as a hero, a spiritualist who saw India as a living goddess, Ma Bhavani Bharati. Modi has often cited Aurobindo in his speeches as a symbol of spiritual and nationalist unity. Following his interactions with a disciple of Sri Aurobindo, Kireet Joshi, Modi believes in Aurobindo's advice about the responsibility of India to share its spiritual wisdom globally. Aurobindo's thinking resonates with that of the Sangh. The Sangh Supremo, Mohan Bhagwat, has said, 'We did not accept Partition then, and we do not accept it today.'

For Narendra Modi, every drop of blood of an Indian soldier is sacred. He has side-stepped impulsive calls from the hotheads including within the BJP and the Sangh Parivar, who give unsolicited advice to end Pakistan's occupation of the PoK, carpet bomb Islamabad, or destroy Pakistan's nuclear installations, to assert India's supremacy. Modi has always taken a statesmanlike approach and prioritized national security. He is conscious that he is dealing with a morbidly irrational enemy, with no checks and balances, and therefore calibrates every strategic decision only with the long-term national interest in mind.

The post-Pahalgam military response of India in May 2025, with its escalatory dynamics, marks a shift in India's military strategy. So far, it was a doctrine of strategic restraint placing priority on avoiding escalation. Narendra Modi has adopted for the first time a strategy of calculated pressure calibrated to avoid a full-scale war but resolved to impose decisive costs on Pakistan. Modi has consciously moved from strategic restraint to punitive deterrence. He has warned Pakistan that henceforth India will no longer make any distinction and hold liable both the terrorists and those who sponsor them, equally. While this may not end Pakistani-sponsored terrorism on Indian soil, it is likely to deter or reduce it.

Pakistan is a rogue State player. Its government has to constantly divert its population's attention from a breakdown of law & order, inflation, and severe economic hardship. Whipping up hatred against India is the only way. Neutral defence analysts estimate that Pakistan has around 170 nuclear warheads. Unlike India, Pakistan's nuclear doctrine states that faced with an existential threat, Islamabad reserves the right to use nuclear weapons, that is, Pakistan explicitly rules out a 'no-first-use' policy. Pakistan has forward-deployed short-range tactical nuclear weapons intended to blunt a significant Indian conventional incursion. Faced with such an existential threat, India may well have to soon review its no-first-use policy and actively seek first-strike capability. Some informal hints have already been dropped to this effect in diplomatic circles. This raises the fear of what defence experts, term as, inadvertent escalation.

Narendra Modi's recent tone and tenor against Pakistan is evidently more strident. Setting up an Iron Dome like indigenously developed air and missile shield to safeguard critical sites and civilians, called Mission Sudarshan Chakra, derived from Lord Krishna's famed divine weapon, the boomerang like disc of assured destruction; to Modi's declared resolve not to concede to Pakistan's nuclear blackmail; to increase nuclear energy tenfold by 2047, are significant steps in a militarily proactive policy. The suspension of the IWT, a non-invasive weapon, will throttle Pakistan's economic lifeline.

A desperate and irrational adversary like Pakistan; having suicide terrorism in its DNA, could, under extreme internal collapse or imminent defeat, or if terrorist groups get hold of its nuclear installations, attempt a form of national suicide by launching a nuclear strike on India. It would seed its own annihilation, but not before plunging India and the entire region into unimaginable catastrophe.

The next few years are therefore extremely critical, as Pakistan totters towards bankruptcy, fragmentation and possible disintegration. India rests in peace knowing that at this critical juncture there is no better guarantee for security than Narendra Modi and his visionary NSA, Doval. Modi hardly sleeps, but India sleeps well, with Modi in command.

CHAPTER TEN

Justice & Justices

EVERY FULL-TERM PRIME Minister of India has had a love-hate relationship with the Supreme Court. Nehru was terribly frustrated with the Supreme Court blocking his agricultural land reforms. Indira Gandhi mauled both the Constitution and the judiciary. Rajiv had to legislate to overturn a problematic Supreme Court judgment, to appease the agitated Muslim clergy. Narasimha Rao was hassled over personal corruption allegations being scrutinized by the Court. Public interest litigation proliferated during the term of Vajpayee, who in his characteristic easy-going style, mumbled something about 'judicial overreach', and then kept quiet. During Dr Manmohan Singh's decade in power, the Supreme Court went into an overdrive, cancelling telecom licenses, de-allocating coal blocks, and was accused by the Congress of 'judicial tyranny' and 'government by judiciary'. Narendra Modi has played it differently.

As a brilliant but opinionated judge of the Supreme Court, Justice V.R. Krishna Iyer, memorably observed in one of his colourful judgements: 'not the Potomac, but the Thames, fertilizes the waters of the Yamuna'. In other words, the executive power in India flows from the Parliament, as in England, and not from the President, as in America. However, the Indian Constitution follows the American Constitution in the matter of judicial review. In England, Parliament is sovereign, and the Courts cannot sit in judgement over legislation passed by the Parliament. In India, as in America, the Supreme Court and the High Courts, can strike down any legislation which is unconstitutional.

Both Ambedkar and Nehru were strongly in favour of inclusion of judicial review, a core feature of the American Constitution. Ambedkar believed that the judiciary must have the power to strike down any law which violates fundamental rights. Many stalwarts, including Govind Ballabh Pant and T.T. Krishnamachari, or popularly, TTK, later Nehru's finance minister, were worried that excessive judicial power could delay or derail social and economic transformation. Ambedkar's position, however prevailed, and the Courts were made the guardians of constitutional morality.

TTK proved prophetic. Post-Independence, Nehru's government launched various laws to abolish *zamindari* to distribute land amongst poor farmers. These laws were challenged in the Courts, as violation of the Right to Property; a fundamental right, under Article 31, at that time. The Supreme Court held that the compensation for acquisition had to be just, judicially reviewable, not merely as decided by the government. Jawaharlal Nehru called the Supreme Court, 'capitalist-minded', 'protecting old landholding elites and blocking the transformative agenda of socialism'. He was indeed right.

In 1950, in Parliament, Nehru defiantly declared: 'If the Constitution comes in the way of our policies for the people, we will change the Constitution.'

Nehru implemented his threat. Within the very first year, Parliament passed various amendments to the Constitution insulating land reforms from judicial review by placing them under the Ninth Schedule to the Constitution.

Thus, trouble began from day one between Nehru's government and the Supreme Court. Although Nehru felt terribly agitated, he gracefully took it in his stride. His daughter had absolutely no such compunction and tamed the judiciary, like an expert ringmaster. Judicial review, she imperiously asserted, certainly did not mean some fancy constitutional lawyers overturning the will of a billion people. None can disagree that the first dramatically serious assault on the Constitution of India and the Supreme Court was launched by Indira Gandhi. Modi's opponents often accuse him and the BJP, of undermining the Constitution. Indira Gandhi did not bother to undermine the Constitution; she simply overwhelmed it.

■

Parameshwaran Mohan Kumaramangalam studied at Eton and Cambridge, read law at Inner Temple, London, and was a brilliant barrister with Marxist ideology. He became a member of the Communist Party of India (CPI). In what came to be popularly known as 'the Kumaramangalam Thesis' or the 'Infiltration Theory', he believed that the way forward for committed leftists and socialists is not by opposing the Indian State from the outside, but by infiltrating and influencing the system from within. He left the CPI and joined Indira's Congress, which was already veering to the left with decisions like nationalisation of public sector banks, and abolition of privy purses of former rulers. He was appointed as the Minister of Steel and Mines, where he promoted nationalization and State control.

In 1967, the Supreme Court, in the case of Golaknath, held that Parliament cannot amend fundamental rights. In 1971, after the liberation of Bangladesh, Indira Gandhi became a national hero and was re-elected with a huge majority. She decided to introduce several constitutional amendments which asserted that Parliament could amend any part of the Constitution, including fundamental rights. She went on to curtail the Right to Property and severely limit judicial review in land acquisition compensation matters, avenging her father's frustration.

Keshavananda Bharati, a Hindu monk, who headed a rich land-owning Kerala monastery, would have his name associated with the most important constitutional decision of the Supreme Court. Bharati and other landowners were highly agitated with the last amendment. A bunch of cases came before the Supreme Court, in which the key question was: Does Parliament have the unlimited power to amend the Constitution, including fundamental rights? The matter would be decided by the largest ever bench of thirteen judges.

Two Parsi lawyers from Mumbai, with formidable reputations, were the gladiators in this judicial battle.

H.M. Seervai, foremost authority on the Constitution of India, a man of saintly integrity, erudite and scholarly, appeared for the State. Nani Palkhivala, eminent income tax expert, silver tongued, who colourfully criticized every annual budget of the Government of India before a packed Brabourne Stadium in Mumbai, a pro-American champion of free enterprise, had challenged every socialistic decision of Indira Gandhi before the Supreme Court, appeared for Keshavananda Bharati and the other Petitioners. Palkhivala would later be appointed by the Janata party government as India's ambassador to the USA, a post from which he had to resign, following a faux pas in which he was photographed on his knees, trying to help President Carter's mother, Lillian, to put on her shoe.

Seervai contended that parliamentary power was unlimited, including the power to amend fundamental rights. He contended that the will of the people, as expressed through Parliament, cannot be curbed by unelected judges. Seervai warned that the 'basic structure' theory would create judicial supremacy and not constitutional supremacy.

Palkhivala argued that Parliament cannot disturb the basic structure of the Constitution and that there were inherent limits to the Parliament's power of amendment. Parliament is only a creature of the Constitution and cannot override its own source of legitimacy. Unlimited amendments will pave the way for totalitarianism.

Six judges agreed with Seervai, and six with Palkhivala.

The 13th Judge, Justice HR Khanna, stated that while the Parliament indeed had unlimited power to amend, it could not amend any feature which constituted a part of the basic structure or core of the Constitution. Khanna's opinion became the law of the land by a narrow majority of 7-6. Mohan Kumaramangalam, the law minister, went berserk. He convinced his boss, Indira, to act ruthlessly. She did not require much convincing anyway.

The Opposition has often accused Narendra Modi and Amit Shah for acting with indecent haste in passing the abrogation of Article 370 and the Citizenship Amendment Laws by the Parliament. Indira Gandhi far outpaced them. The Keshavananda Bharati judgement was pronounced on April 24, 1973, and the Chief Justice of India (CJI) Sikri, retired on the very next day, April 25. So far, by convention, the senior-most judge of the Supreme Court had always been appointed to the dominant position of the CJI who steers the Court in the direction he wants. The CJI is not only 'first amongst equals.' Increasingly, he shapes the functioning of the entire Court.

The three senior-most judges to take over from Sikri were Justices Shelat, Hegde and Grover, all of whom had decided against the government. Indira Gandhi decided to supersede them overnight and appointed the judge fourth in seniority, Justice A. N. Ray, as the CJI. This was the beginning of what Kumaramangalam called 'committed judiciary'. A judiciary ideologically aligned to the socialistic agenda of the government and not merely committed to legal formalism. The battering of the Supreme Court had begun. Within five weeks, Mohan Kumaramangalam died in an air crash. He was 56. Many decades later, his son would be a BJP minister, who was highly regarded as a rising star in political circles and whose life was tragically cut short at 48, by leukemia.

Later in 1975, the Supreme Court (Justice Krishna Iyer) hit back at Indira by granting her only a conditional stay of the Allahabad High Court judgement, which had invalidated her election to the Lok Sabha, and had placed curbs on her functioning. There has been intense speculation, even by bitter critics of Indira Gandhi, that the Supreme Court ought to have granted a full stay of the Allahabad High Court judgement, whatever the merits of the case, and had such stay been granted, perhaps, and it is a very big perhaps, Indira may not have declared the Emergency, which she did, that very night. Years later, the judge himself said that it would have been better to have granted a full stay.

This was a classic case of an Indian court (Justice Sinha of the Allahabad High Court), in a rush of adrenaline, unseating a long-standing Prime Minister for procedural violations, in an election where her opponent had forfeited his security deposit, and unwittingly setting in motion horrendous consequences for the Republic. Assuming that each violation that was alleged had indeed occurred, it would not have made any difference to the ultimate result of the election. However, the judge, reportedly of impeccable integrity, took a narrow technical view and ignored the substance. In such supercharged political decisions, you do not require a purist; you require a pragmatist.

As soon as the Emergency was declared, the Supreme

Court waved the white flag to the Indira government. The judiciary surrendered to Indira Gandhi like a docile lamb, barring a couple of heroic exceptions.

During the Emergency, Indira Gandhi suspended fundamental rights, including the right to life and liberty. Several opposition leaders and activists were arrested without trial, which led to their families filing habeas corpus petitions before the Supreme Court. In the celebrated case of ADM Jabalpur v. Shivkant Shukla, the Supreme Court, by a majority of 4 to 1, held that 'during an Emergency, when Article 21 is suspended, no person has the right to approach any court for setting aside unlawful detention.' In other words, when the government suspended it, no right to life or liberty can exist, and no Court can question the order of the executive on preventive detention. Once again, Justice H.R. Khanna was the only dissenting voice. This has been termed as 'the blackest hour' of the Supreme Court. One of the sitting judges of the Supreme Court wrote a letter to Indira Gandhi, stating that: 'You have become the symbol of the hopes and aspirations of the poor, hungry millions of Indians who had so far nothing to hope for and nothing to live for. Today the reddish glow of the rising sun is holding out the promise of a bright sunshine. May that sunshine fill our hearts with joy and bring comfort and cheer to the poor, half-naked, hungry millions of our countrymen.' The nadir of India's judiciary had been reached.

Despite his no-nonsense personality and being more consistently popular than Indira Gandhi, Narendra Modi has never adopted Indira's confrontational approach towards the judiciary.

Post the Godhra riots, the Supreme Court appointed a SIT headed by a brilliant IPS Officer of impeccable integrity, R.K. Raghavan, who had successfully served as Director of the CBI, to investigate whether the Gujarat government administration including Narendra Modi, were in any manner complicit in the riots. The SIT had extensive powers of investigation and evidence gathering. The SIT interrogated Modi for more than nine hours, in 2010, when the Congress was in power. At all stages, Modi fully cooperated with the Supreme Court and SIT. The SIT exonerated Modi of every charge of complicity. The Supreme Court unanimously confirmed all findings of the SIT.

▪

The all-important question of who should appoint the judges of the Supreme Court and the High Courts has plagued successive governments, both Congress and BJP. After the Constitution came in force in 1950, for a period of 23 years thereafter, higher judicial appointments were always made according to the recommendations of the CJI. In April 1973, Indira tossed this convention out of the window, as described above. When the Janata Party government came in power at the Centre, it initially restored the seniority convention but later itself started to transfer High Court Judges who were politically inconvenient.

Indira soon returned to power. Her contempt for the judiciary was well-known. She vigorously continued transferring High Court Judges without their consent which led to what has come to be known as The Three Judges Case.

In the first of these cases, in 1981, a seven-member Constitutional Bench of the Supreme Court (judgment written by Justice P.N. Bhagwati) held that the government has the final say in judicial appointments. However, in the Second Judges Case, in 1993, when Narasimha Rao was in power, the Supreme Court overruled its own judgement and created the Collegium System comprising of the Chief Justice of India and two seniormost Supreme Court Judges. In 1998, the Collegium was expanded to four seniormost Supreme Court Judges and the Chief Justice of India. Hence, at present, this Collegium of five makes recommendations to the Central Government which may return them once for reconsideration by the Collegium, however, if the Collegium once again reconfirms, the Government is bound to accept such a recommendation.

In America, it is common practice for every President to fill up vacancies in the Supreme Court by judges who are ideologically inclined with the political views of the President and his party, that is, conservative or liberal. Many, therefore, consider the US Supreme Court as partisan and polarized.

While India adopted the American system of judicial review, it did not adopt the American system of the executive (President) filling in the vacancies on the Supreme Court by appointing judges (to be confirmed by the Senate). Many believe that there is a rationale underlying the American system that if the judges are to have such wide powers to review legislation, then they should be appointed by the executive, and confirmed by the legislature, a fine balance between the three branches of the State. In India, the power of judicial review coupled with the Collegium System has the potential for serious confrontation between the self-appointing judiciary on the one hand, and the executive and the legislature, on the other.

Can unelected judges curb the will of the people. And when judges themselves appoint judges, isn't it a recipe for continuance of the so-called 'old boys' club or the status quo. Do all judges have the intellectual capacity and the financial literacy to grasp highly complex economic and financial issues. Brilliant lawyers with lucrative practice seldom opt for the bench where the remuneration is not even 0.5% of the professional fees earned by senior lawyers. While increasingly tribunals with expert knowledge, determine complex matters; at the level of the Supreme Court and the High Courts, no such technical expertise or domain knowledge is always available. Judges have to resist the carrot and stick approach adopted by successive governments in dangling attractive positions post-retirement on the implicit understanding that they fall in line with the party in power.

After Narendra Modi became PM on May 24, 2014, in August of that year, the Parliament passed the 99th Constitutional Amendment Act and the National Judicial Appointment Commission Act which sought to replace the Collegium System by appointments of judges by the government and some eminent persons. It is extremely relevant to note that these legislations were passed by a unanimous decision in the Lok Sabha (including Congress voting in favour) of 367 votes in favour and none against;

and in the Rajya Sabha with 179 votes in favour against the lone dissenting vote of Ram Jethmalani. Thus the 99th amendment had the unanimous backing of all political parties and complied with the strict requirements of majority stipulated by the Constitution including ratification by more than twenty states. This was a rare event in the legislative history of India where the bitterest political opponents had all united to effect such a change.

However, the Supreme Court of India, in a spirit of defiance, struck down the 99th Amendment in October 2015, by a majority of 4:1. As someone quipped, it was like turkey cancelling Christmas. The Modi government filed a review petition post this judgment, which too, was dismissed in December 2018. Two eminent Supreme Court lawyers, across the political spectrum, minced no words. BJP's Arun Jaitley called it a 'tyranny of the unelected'. Abhishek Manu Singhvi of the Congress said that 'it reflects a worrying trend of judicial supremacy overriding the will of parliament and the states'.

Despite the overruling of such unanimous legislative will, Narendra Modi did not adopt any aggressive or confrontational approach against the Supreme Court, even though on this issue, the entire political spectrum was behind him. What seemed like a setback for the Modi government was a tactical retreat by Narendra Modi. Against Indira's committed judiciary, Narendra Modi avoided confrontation which led to a harmoniously functioning judiciary.

Judicial activism by the Supreme Court has led to admirable socioeconomic reform. Whenever the other two branches of the government, the legislature and the executive, have failed to discharge their duties, the Supreme Court has proactively upheld rights and interpreted laws to advance justice. In Vishakha vs. State of Rajasthan, (1997), the Supreme Court laid down sexual harassment guidelines even before Parliament enacted the law, which was an extremely salutary measure.

However, when judicial activism degenerates into judicial overreach, a constitutional crisis results. Examples of judicial overreach are manifold, which upsets the legislature and the executive, and every party across the political spectrum. In 2013, cancellation of the coal blocks allocation led to severe economic disruption. Recently, the overturning of the multi-billion-dollar sale transaction in the Bhushan Power and Steel case has created horrendous difficulties for all concerned including the banks and financial institutions. Similarly, the Supreme Court striking down the 99th Constitutional Amendment despite the unanimous will of the people as expressed by Parliament was a glaring example of judicial overreach. Banning firecrackers to curb air pollution during Diwali or liquor sales within 500 meters of national highways, two undoubtedly excellent decisions to protect the public interest, nevertheless amounts to law-making by the judiciary.

In the interaction with the Collegium, the government of the day has a distinct advantage. The former is a constantly changing body with judges retiring when they reach 65. Since it comprises of the CJI and the four seniormost judges, most of them are on the verge of retirement, and hence its composition is in a state of constant flux. If there is an uncomfortable Collegium, the government has to simply wait. Like the English weather, the Collegium will soon change. If the government strongly disagrees with the recommendation made by the Collegium, it either resends the file to the Collegium or simply sits on it for several months. At times, the government shares the result of the check carried out by the Intelligence Bureau on the proposed appointee with the Collegium, which then reflects upon the material furnished and often withdraws its recommendation. And the government is on high moral ground here. The entire nation, whose will as reflected by a unanimous Parliament, did not want to continue with the Collegium system. Despite this, the Supreme Court persisted with this system of appointment.

Also, while on the face of it, this looks like a public confrontation between the judiciary and the legislature-executive, in practical terms, the system has not worked badly. A consensus view emerges amongst the Chief Justice and senior judges of a High Court that a particular Advocate ought to be asked if he is interested in becoming a judge. Unfortunately, as the remuneration of a judge is grossly inadequate, barring a very public-spirited advocate, those who have a large practice, usually spurn the offer. While several judges are indeed intellectually brilliant, generally speaking, the best legal minds are seldom seen on the bench. The proposed appointee then undergoes a vigorous background check by the police and the IB. Vigilance continues to be maintained to prevent corruption in the judiciary. Critics of the system submit that this leads to a pressurized judiciary which may not want to go against the government in a critical matter having serious political repercussions. The government, therefore, in practice, continues to retain indirect control over judicial appointments, even under a Collegium system. A possible reason why attempts have not been made by any political party to restore the 99th Amendment.

Narendra Modi keeps an eye on pending recommendations of the Collegium only to ensure that the nation does not lose a good judge for the wrong reasons. He is aware of most transfers and elevations. In the annual meeting, the President of India and the Prime Minister have with all the Chief Justices of the High Courts, Modi remembers the name and background of each Chief Justice. Since several of them would be elevated to the Supreme Court, the Prime Minister is aware about the profile of most future Supreme Court judges. No wonder Narendra Modi sleeps for only four hours every day.

The Modi government was legally vindicated by the Supreme Court in two cases of immense ideological and emotional importance to the BJP and Modi. Although it took little more than four years, the Supreme Court Constitutional Bench unanimously upheld the power of the President to extinguish Article 370 (Kashmir) and the power of the Parliament to reorganize a state. BJP's most important ideological move was unanimously conferred judicial legitimacy.

The litigation around the Ram Janma Bhoomi case had lingered for an incredible 134 years (1885-2019). Nine years had elapsed even after the Supreme Court admitted an appeal against the Allahabad High Court judgement. There appeared to be no hurry to fix the final hearing. A final high-profile mediation had failed.

In February 2019, a former Supreme Court judge, Justice Katju, hinted at serious allegations of impropriety against CJI Ranjan Gogoi, his lawyer son-in-law and the latter's father, a High Court judge. In April 2019, the Gujarat Bar Association too demanded an inquiry about these allegations. In the same month, sexual harassment allegations made on an affidavit by a staff member surfaced against the CJI. Although he ultimately got a clean chit, the CJI was a shaken man. He was due to retire on 17th November 2019. If he could deliver a judgement in this most high-profile case before his retirement, he would go out on a high note.

The CJI scheduled day-to-day hearings of the Ram Janmabhoomi case which went on continuously for an unprecedented 40 days from 6th August 2019 and ended on 16 October. Within 24 days of the completion of the arguments and only 8 days before the CJI's retirement, the five-member bench unanimously awarded the entire land of 2.77 acres for the Ram Mandir. Modi had worked tirelessly with the Government's law officers in their preparations for arguments in the Ram Mandir case and provided critical sociopolitical insights.

Gogoi was nominated as a Member of Parliament (Rajya Sabha) within four months of his retirement. Justice Katju though was most displeased and publicly made some denigrating references to the former CJI.

Within just 24 days of the completion of arguments

which had lasted 40 days, to deliver a 1045 page judgement, which was intellectually brilliant and superbly structured, was nothing short of a miracle. By all accounts, Justice Dhananjay Chandrachud, who would later become the CJI, was that miracle man.

Chandrachud authored several brilliant judgments, both before and after he became CJI. Privacy was declared a fundamental right, overturning precedent. Similarly, his judgments relating to decriminalization of homosexuality and transgender-heterosexual marriages were appreciated as being finely balanced.

During his tenure as CJI, he generally enjoyed a cordial relationship with the Modi government, though he strongly voiced his agitation over the government holding up judicial appointments recommended by the Collegium headed by him, publicly calling it 'an executive veto'.

Narendra Modi accepted Chandrachud's invitation to visit the latter's official residence to participate in a private Ganesh Pooja ceremony on September 11, 2024. This was not the first time that a CJI had invited a prime minister to attend a private function. It was widely and transparently publicized on Narendra Modi's social media channels and yet some opposition leaders alleged that such a visit compromised judicial independence and suggested that the CJI should recuse himself from cases involving the government. Some legal commentators and judges too were critical that such a visit may impact public perception of judicial impartiality. Significantly, this visit was less than nine weeks before Chandrachud's retirement.

It was Justice Chandrachud again who headed a five-judge bench, which unanimously struck down the Electoral Bond Scheme, introduced in January 2018, as unconstitutional and violative of fundamental rights. Under this Scheme, it had become permissible for citizens or corporates to donate anonymously to political parties. The Supreme Court judgement resulted in immediate suspension of the Scheme and the Election Commission of India had to disclose the details of the donations and the donees to the public.

This judgement was the only major judicial reverse suffered by the Modi government. It was delivered weeks before the start of the 2024 national elections and days before the Model Code of Conduct came into force.

During his third term, the Modi government has so far not attempted to reintroduce the Electoral Bonds Scheme in a modified form, in accordance with the Supreme Court guidelines. After delivering two crucial judgements in favour of the Modi government—Article 370 and Ram Mandir—and then by striking down the Electoral Bonds Scheme, Justice Chandrachud had demonstrated his judicial independence and impartiality.

Unlike Indira Gandhi's openly hostile approach to the judiciary and scant regard for the Constitution, Narendra Modi adopted a strategic and nuanced approach. Until he became the Chief Minister of Gujarat in 2001, Modi had no significant interaction with the courts. Post the 2002 riots, the Supreme Court, in 2003, moved the criminal trials out of Gujarat and began to monitor the investigations. It went on to appoint the SIT with extremely wide powers to investigate.

Narendra Modi maintained decorum and institutional respect for the Supreme Court, except for mildly criticizing the 'judicial overreach'. Ultimately, the Supreme Court not only upheld the SIT findings which unconditionally exonerated him from all charges but also held that the petitioners were politically motivated and not entirely honest.

Modi's style of operation vis-à-vis the Collegium has been subtle and diplomatic. While his government accepted most of the recommendations of the Collegium, it rejected a few for valid reasons which were conveyed to the Collegium in confidence. Considering that the entire country wanted to replace the Collegium system, Modi government's tactics are legitimate and have not offended the dignity of the Supreme Court.

Indira's bulldozer approach with the judiciary will be contrasted by historians with Narendra Modi's quietly working in a spirit of co-operation with the judiciary. He has always been reticent to speak in public about the judiciary and proved himself to be a masterly operator in his dealings with the Justices.

A country which does not pay its judges adequately is being extremely short-sighted. This has led to issues of mediocrity and probity which has shaken the confidence of the judiciary. It has made the life of an upright judge difficult. It has shaken the confidence of the litigants in the judiciary to deliver justice. When courts attempt to substitute their own judgement for the political judgement of a duly elected government, the judicial overreach creates a dangerous confrontation. Narendra Modi is extremely conscious of the systemic fault lines in the delivery of justice. This writer would not be surprised if some far-reaching judicial reforms are on the anvil.

CHAPTER ELEVEN

Black is Not Beautiful

LATE EVENING OF 8th November 2016, at 7.55 p.m. IST, as the world watched with disbelief, the emerging possibility of Donald Trump pulling off a stunning upset victory over the hot favourite Hillary Clinton in the American presidential elections, Narendra Modi walked into an ante room next to a television studio and greeted a few of his senior cabinet ministers sitting there and speculating why they had been summoned by the Prime Minister at this late hour, who blandly told them that he was about to make an important national announcement.

Sharp at 8 p.m., the Prime Minister began to speak about how corruption and black money had spread their tentacles due to self-serving businessmen, politicians and officials who had ignored the poor, and cornered benefits. 'For years, said the Prime Minister, this country has felt that corruption, black money and terrorism are festering sores, holding us back in the race towards development' and 'the time has come for a strong and decisive step'. Narendra Modi paused significantly and then announced, that ₹500 and ₹1000 currency notes presently in use will no longer be legal tender from midnight. 86% of the total currency notes in circulation stood instantly demonetized. What exactly had made Modi drop the D-Bomb on an unsuspecting nation, including his ministers waiting in the anteroom.

Post Independence, Nehruvian socialistic planning of the Indian economy had resulted in the Licence Raj. Industry, whether small, medium or big, requires obtaining dozens of scattered licenses and permissions before commencing manufacturing. Like in a Kafka novel, if you were too successful and exceeded your installed industrial capacity, you faced civil and criminal penalties. A corollary of the Licence Raj was the Inspector Raj, which led to bribery and bureaucratic corruption. There was underreporting of production to avoid excise duty, sales tax and income tax. For decades, liquor barons derived their obscene profits only from avoiding excise duty and selling alcohol in cash.

When Yashwantrao Balwantrao Chavan was the finance minister in Indira Gandhi's government in the early 1970s, the maximum marginal rate of income tax reached 97.5% which led to the absurd situation that an honest taxpayer had to borrow to pay taxes which exceeded 104%, due to the incidence of wealth tax coupled with income tax. Estate, or death duty, was levied at an expropriatory rate of 85% on estates valued above ₹20 lakhs. This led to tax evasion becoming a rule rather than an exception.

Gold was smuggled in dhows from the Gulf and sold for cash in the black market. The hawala system flourished and taxi drivers sold dollars and pounds ('drill' and 'poplin' in street lingo) on cash in the streets of Mumbai and Delhi. In 2011, it was reported that Indians had billions stashed in Swiss and other foreign bank deposits. Stamp duty rates for transactions of immovable property were far below the market rates, leading to heavy use of cash in buying and selling real estate. Small traders and professionals paid virtually no tax. Enforcement of tax laws was weak and riddled with corruption. Some business houses were notorious not only for financing the promoter's share of the equity of a new project but also creating a nest egg for the promoter family, out of the kickbacks they received abroad from foreign suppliers or service providers for the project, whose cost was padded up.

Elections were won by political parties distributing cash to buy votes which led to a lack of political will to reform the system. The typical Asian benami practice of holding assets in someone else's name to conceal real ownership was widespread and laws enacted to deal with such practices were not effectively enforced. In the absence of digital infrastructure, cash was king, and money laundering was rampant. Through shell companies, bogus IPOs and circular trading, Stock Exchanges had become the new Wild West for money laundering.

Up to 1999/2000, it was a criminal offense to hold assets abroad without declaring to Indian tax, punishable with imprisonment under the draconian Foreign Exchange Regulation Act, which was replaced by the benign Foreign Exchange Management Act under which there was only civil, and not criminal, liability.

In 1985, Rajiv Gandhi's Finance Minister, V.P. Singh initiated tax reforms such as abolition of estate duty and reduced tax rates to encourage compliance. Dr Manmohan Singh, both as Finance Minister and Prime Minister, rationalized tax slabs and introduced reforms which proved inadequate to address the problem. Some unofficial estimates for the share of the black economy in India's GDP ranged as high as 45% to 62%.

During Dr Singh's Prime Ministership (2004 to 2014), there were 25 major Islamic terror attacks sponsored by Pakistan's ISI which started circulating counterfeit currency in states like Kashmir and Punjab to sponsor terrorism. The UPA government had strongly resisted the Supreme Court's direction to form a Special Investigation Team (SIT) to investigate black money. Black was indeed beautiful.

As soon as he assumed office, Narendra Modi, in keeping with his election manifesto, devised a master plan to combat black money after speaking to many economists and tax experts. In the very first cabinet meeting, it was resolved to immediately operationalize a SIT to investigate black money as promised in the BJP manifesto. This was followed by the Parliament passing the Black Money (Undisclosed Foreign Income and Assets) Act, 2015.

Narendra Modi's resolve to drastically reduce, if not eliminate black money, was sincere. For the first time, the Indian taxpayer realized that the government was deadly serious and that none would be spared. The whole initiative was driven personally by Modi and his office. The nation came to believe, for the first time, that it would no longer be business as usual.

Narendra Modi's Anti-Black Money Playbook adopted a 'carrot and stick' approach. In 2015, before the Black Money Act came into force, taxpayers were allowed to voluntarily disclose and pay tax, resulting in a disclosure of ₹4147 crores. Before demonetization, Modi launched the most successful Tax Amnesty Program in India's history for a period of four months for taxpayers to disclose unaccounted assets including cash, gold, jewellery, real estate, shares and foreign bank accounts. Tax was payable at 45% of the disclosed income. A total amount of ₹65,250 crores was declared. Just after demonetization, another Tax Amnesty Scheme was introduced from 17th December 2016 upto 31st March 2017 under which black money declared would be channelized into welfare investments, with tax liability at 50% of the declared income. In addition, 25% of the declared income had to be compulsorily deposited in a government welfare scheme, locked in for four years without interest. ₹4900 crores were declared and used mostly for girl education and social welfare. In 2019, under the Legacy Dispute Resolution Scheme, to resolve pre-GST disputes, ₹39,000 crores were declared.

The Black Money Act was the legislative framework for effectively initiating action. The tax amnesty schemes were a final opportunity to come clear before the fireworks began. It was time now that the system was given a shock by demonetization of high value notes.

Contrary to what critics alleged, the Prime Minister had been exhaustively briefed about the pros and cons of demonetization and the temporary disruption and chaos, it was bound to cause. However, he and a tight knit circle of advisors concluded, after a detailed risk reward analysis, that demonetization was a necessary weapon in the armoury to combat black money. Its main purpose was to strike fear in the minds of the hoarder of unaccounted cash. It would accelerate the digitalization of the Indian economy. Within a few months of demonetization, the government would launch GST which would make cash transactions, commercially unviable. Demonetization would jangle the nerves of the tax evader who would be left guessing as to what will come next. It was the shock and fear factor, an act of symbolic cleansing. Utmost secrecy was the key to success and time was running out. The government knew that no major windfall would occur to the government from the unreturned currency. In any event, that was never the objective. Apart from tax evasion, demonetization would strike a decisive blow against ISI circulating counterfeit notes in Kashmir and other states.

Modi decided to consult the then RBI Governor, Dr Raghuram Rajan, under whose remit demonetization fell.

Rajan, a highly respected economist, had served as a Chief Economist at IMF. In 2012, the Manmohan Singh government appointed him as its Chief Economic Advisor and, in August 2013, as the Governor of the Reserve Bank of India. An inflation hawk, he endeavoured to clean up the banking sector, forcing banks to recognize stressed assets, as also set the stage for the Monetary Policy Committee to depoliticize interest rate decisions.

Despite Rajan being a UPA appointee, Narendra Modi forged a warm relationship with him and had several sessions with him to tap his wisdom. When Modi asked his views on demonetization, Rajan stated that he believed that the disruption which would be caused by the measure would outweigh long term advantages. Rajan had a formidable reputation for being prophetic. In 2005, he had warned the Annual Symposium of the World's finance ministers at Jackson Hole of a global financial crisis looming large. He proved to be deadly accurate when the crisis did happen in 2008–09. Modi's style has always been to consult experts and assimilate the advice but then take his own decision.

Rajan has had a soft corner for the Congress. His term was to expire on 4th September 2016. Rajan voluntarily informed the Modi government that he was not interested in a second term as he wanted to return to academia. It was widely reported that Rajan was the choice of the Congress for being the shadow finance minister in 2019.

Dr Urjit Patel, Rajan's deputy and another former IMF economist, apparently did not share his boss' intellectual opposition to demonetization and was appointed as the new RBI governor, during whose term, demonetization was announced.

Modi knew that demonetization was a huge gamble. Elections were due in the politically important state of Uttar Pradesh (UP) within a few months. The informal or unorganized sector in India was nearly 85%, and it relied heavily on cash. For a few months, demonetization was certain to cause considerable distress and disruption in this informal sector. The small traders and businessmen, mostly likely to be affected, were the BJP's most valuable voter base. However, Narendra Modi's contrarian thinking was that even though the common man would temporarily be harassed, he would be politically perceptive enough to appreciate that Modi's move, was giving more sleepless nights to the tax evading rich and would ultimately benefit the country. It would also demonstrate that Modi practiced what he preached and that his election promise, to launch a relentless onslaught on black money, was not hollow.

In the UP elections, the BJP won a landslide victory by gaining 312 out of 403 seats. Ajay Singh Bisht, who would soon be known to the world, as Yogi Adityanath, a firebrand young Hindu monk and activist, cast in Narendra Modi's mould, became the new Chief Minister. The backward and rural classes, severely affected by the demonetization and who had suffered considerably, nevertheless voted heavily for the BJP. Modi's political gamble had paid off handsomely.

Modi was not the first to demonetize. On 12th January 1946, the British India government had demonetized ₹1000, ₹5000 and ₹10000 notes to target counterfeit currencies and black money. Post the Emergency, Morarji Desai's Janata government, on 16th January 1978, had demonetized ₹1000, ₹5000 and ₹10000 notes by passing a legislation. Such high denomination notes were then not being widely used by the public and the disruption was therefore minimal.

The ₹10000 note has had an interesting journey. Printed by the Reserve Bank of India in 1938, it was reintroduced in 1954 and demonetized in 1978. Rumours continue to circulate of its imminent reincarnation including a high-tech version emitting a digital signal, when stored beyond a certain quantity.

Short term disruption is inevitable in any demonetization exercise; and this was a massive exercise, the biggest ever in the world, involving 86% of currency notes in circulation, overnight ceasing to be legal tender; and affecting 1.4 billion people. India has the largest informal or unorganized sector in the world which heavily depended on cash. This sector, along with agriculture and daily wage workers, had to bear the acute pain of this exercise for nearly five months. For the last quarter of FY 2017, the GDP growth slid from 8% to 6.1% and an estimated 15 lakhs jobs were lost.

As soon as Modi announced demonetization, frantic cash hoarders rushed to gold traders to exchange cash for gold, only to find the doors of the shops locked. From the next morning, for several weeks, nationwide serpentine queues formed outside banks, to exchange old notes. The unemployed youth made good money by acting as mules for the rich. Like in most Asian countries, there is no stigma attached to unaccounted cash in India, and people found novel ways to get rid of the demonetized notes. From industrialists to housewives to politicians to bureaucrats to realtors to professionals, caught unawares by Modi's move, frantically scrambled to carry out one of the world's largest mass money laundering operations. Farmland was dug up in the middle of the night to excavate bundles of currency notes buried there, as evident from the soiled notes deposited with the banks. Ultimately 99.3% of the demonetized currency notes were returned. More than what was expected.

In their desperate hurry to deposit old notes, many false tax declarations were made. Post demonetization, 'Operation

Clean Money 2017', was launched by the tax department by using data analytics of 1.8 crore post-demo accounts and investigations launched into the genuineness of those who had declared 'cash on hand', who were asked to explain the source, which many could not.

In order to rapidly replenish the currency after the demonetization of ₹500 and ₹1000 notes, the Government introduced new pink colored ₹2000 notes, not intended for long term circulation. Accordingly, its printing was stopped in 2018-19 and these notes were 'mini-demonetized' or 'withdrawn'. 97.9% of such notes were returned by August 2024. During the short period the ₹2000 notes remained in circulation, they became a convenient method of hoarding cash. Nevertheless, in the public mind, this mini demonetization created further fear that there could be other such demonetizations in the future.

In 2025, nine years after demonetization, the parallel or black money economy, has a much smaller share of the GDP. Estimating the size of a shadow economy in a country like India is an extremely difficult exercise. However, conservative economic studies suggest that pre-demonetization, it was estimated at 17.22% of GDP which stood reduced to 13.6% in 2025. The currency in circulation (CiC)-to-GDP ratio reduced from 12.5% (FY23) to 11.1% (FY25). The number of income tax filers increased from 5.48 crores to 9 crores. In the very first quarter after demonetization, as much as 1.01 crores of new income tax filers applied to come on record. The criteria of 'informal sector cash use' which was estimated at 45% of the retail value is estimated to have reduced to 25%

in 2025. Net direct tax to GDP rose from 5.62% to 6.7%.

Despite the above, Modi's critics have gleefully labelled demonetization as a policy failure and a Delhi to Daulatabad kind of decision. Dispassionate economic studies will record it as a trigger point for acceleration of the digital economy in India and a launching pad for the most far-reaching tax reforms. The ecosystem of taxation in India was hardcore cynical when Modi took office. Successive governments had waxed eloquent about combating black money and had done little about it. Narendra Modi was determined to shake the system out of its complacency. He had to signal to India that he meant business and would be ruthless with tax evaders. Demonetization put the fear of God in them. It was a theatrical display of State power. This decision was responsible for focusing the attention of the entire nation, from billionaire to beggar, on the problem of black money. From the richest industrialist to the housewife to children, everyone knew that suddenly old notes had lost their value. Modi had urged the masses to bear the distress for 50 days in a collective ritual of sacrifice. The people had responded. Modi's personal pristine clean record strengthened the anti-evasion narrative.

As planned, the Modi government, after the shock treatment of demonetization, rapidly introduced a flurry of anti-avoidance and anti-evasion measures. Extensive income tax searches unearthed a staggering ₹1.38 lakh crores (USD 15 billion) of undisclosed income. The implementation of the Black Money Act made non-compliant taxpayers extremely nervous. Most of them had suffered a serious loss due to demonetization having compelled to bear the 'unofficial conversion cost' (ranging between 10% to 25%) for laundering unaccounted cash. The melodrama of the demonetization announcement frayed nerves. Thereafter, every time it was announced that the Prime Minister would address the nation, many politicians and businessmen became nervous. The mindset of the evader, that it would be business as usual, had been rudely shattered. This is exactly what Modi wanted.

The Benami Transactions (Prohibition) Act enacted in 1988 had remained toothless. It was drastically amended in 2017, resulting in assets worth thousands of crores being attached, and prosecutions launched. The Companies Act was amended to make mandatory disclosure of a 'warm body' (individual) as the ultimate beneficial owner of shares.

More than 130 criminal prosecutions were initiated against 4200+ Indian residents whose names appeared as illegal foreign bank account holders in the Panama Papers, Paradise Papers and Swiss bank leaks like HSBC. In 2017, in order to reform the political financial system, Electoral Bonds were introduced. The introduction of the Faceless Assessment Scheme 2020, under which the assessee is not aware who is the assessing officer has led to reduced corruption and harassment of honest taxpayers. Of course, several loopholes still remain in this Scheme which are being addressed.

GST was contemplated as early as 2000, when the Vajpayee government was in power. However, it required Modi's perseverance and political will to enable a quick national launch in July 2017 inspired by the concept of 'one nation, one tax, one market'. The confusing mess of 17 taxes and 13 cesses were merged into a single tax of GST. After a short-term disruption, and the national sport of grumbling about any new change, GST has been truly welcomed by trade and business in avoiding multiple or cascading taxation. Behind the scenes handling of negotiations with the state governments including those ruled by opposition parties, was a minefield, which was cleared in a record time. This was principally attributable to Modi's day-to-day follow up and persuasion including his warm personal equation with the Chief Ministers of opposition-ruled states. GST is a continuous, systemic reform that curbs tax evasion, forces invoice-level transparency and brings entire supply chains under scrutiny.

In 2017, when GST was launched, there were 65 lakh taxpayers which increased to 1.46 crores in FY 2024. Real time e-invoice and e-way bill trails made large scale cash transactions rare and widened the tax base. The launching of GST has made it commercially unviable to carry out bogus transactions in cash. With a maximum income tax rate of 30% (25% for corporates), it no longer makes commercial sense to pay GST @ 18% and cash 'conversion rate' of 8% to 10% for bogus 'entries' or 'loans'; and take the risk of tax evasion with its attendant criminal consequences. It is far more sensible instead to pay tax at 25% or 30%. Further, such person loses the opportunity to officially invest in assets which are able to provide a handsome return on investment. If you lent in cash, and the borrower defaults, you had no legal remedy, unless you happened to be the mafia. People are learning that mattresses are made for sleeping, not for storing cash.

Another deadly blow was struck against black money by the world's largest and most rapid digitalization of the economy. India has the largest number of digital payments in the world today leaving an audit trail which has minimized the use of cash. Digital payments have touched the life of every Indian, and in the years to come, user of cash will become minimal.

Nevertheless, on Indian roads, one can still find a Lamborghini or a Ferrari along with a bullock cart. This 'paradox of co-existence' is still evident in the economy. The world's largest and fastest growing digital payment system (UPI), in July 2025, enjoyed a share of 85% of digital transaction volumes in India. Despite this, cash still remains king in rural areas and in certain informal sectors. Gold bars are still secreted away along with diamonds and precious stones.

With the Supreme Court striking down the Electoral Bonds Scheme as unconstitutional, the use of cash in political funding is bound to increase. Purchase of luxury items like expensive watches and jewellery is another area for parking black money. Small businesses resort to splitting businesses in different names to avoid GST thresholds, where cash usage is still prevalent. GST authorities often have to tackle bogus or false invoices.

Around 2010-12, most major countries except USA adhered to the Common Reporting Standard (CRS) and Automatic Exchange of Information. If a tax resident of

India had a Swiss bank account, the bank had to report to the Swiss tax department which sent the information to the Indian income tax authorities. Combined with the passing of the Black Money Act, this worldwide development put the fear of God in Indian tax residents who had undeclared assets abroad. Many became NRIs by staying out of India for more than 182 days and showing that they were employed abroad. Such NRIs came to be popularly known as 'Modi NRIs', those who had changed their residential status after Narendra Modi became Prime Minister. Tax evasion was fast becoming an inconvenient and costly affair.

Mauritius, Singapore and Cyprus enjoyed the most beneficial Double Taxation Avoidance Agreements (DTAA) with India, which were abused by tax evaders engaging in 'round-tripping' and 'treaty shopping' under which undeclared money generated abroad or sent from India was brought back into India by indulging into structured, circuitous transactions, through shell entities considered tax resident in these countries in order to launder the money as also to minimize payment of tax by availing the concessional rates of tax under the DTAA. The Modi government revised these treaties to plug loopholes. Consequently, FDI routed from Mauritius fell from 34% to 17% in 2024.

After the high profile and dramatic escapades from India of liquor baron Vijay Mallya and diamond traders, Nirav Modi and Mehul Choksi, the Modi Government enacted the Fugitive Economic Offenders Act, 2018 under which 14 persons were declared fugitive economic offenders and assets worth several thousand crores confiscated.

Since decades, tax evaders have laundered money and evaded taxes by incorporating thousands of shell companies, a long-standing practice, in order to obfuscate the ultimate beneficial owner. Various exotic structures were employed such as 'snake-tail-into-mouth' structure under which companies A, B and C held shares in each other, with no natural person as a shareholder. Other structures involved having thousands of such shell companies having the same directors, shareholders and registered offices in unknown locations to avoid scrutiny. The income tax department launched a dramatic assault on the shell company structure by striking off 3.7 lakhs companies out of which 2.25 lakhs were shell companies and blacklisting 4.5 lakhs directors and initiating prosecution under the Benami Prohibition laws.

The Modi government has been accused of weaponising investigative agencies like Central Bureau of Investigation, Enforcement Directorate, Income-tax department, Serious Fraud Office and National Investigation Agency, by selectively targeting opposition leaders, with the object of making them defect to the BJP or toe the government line on critical political issues. Once they defect to the BJP, the heat is off, the critics allege, dubbing it as going through a 'washing machine'.

In almost each of such high-profile corruption or tax evasion cases, courts including the Supreme Court have found sufficient legal merit in the case of the prosecution, to deny bail to the accused; and the Courts have refused to quash proceedings at the very outset, as being an abuse of the process of law. Opposition leaders of impeccable integrity, despite being vocal critics of the Modi government, have had no such cases initiated against them. The higher judiciary has been unsparing of these agencies whenever gross abuse of power has been found. All these political accused are represented by the best available legal talent in the country and yet have had to spend considerable time in jail without bail. Hence, the legal basis of most of these actions is sound in the preliminary scrutiny by the Courts. Some of these scams like the Fodder Scam or the Land-for-Jobs scam or the Delhi liquor policy scam have such glaring facts in the public domain that, on the face of it, the action appears to be not politically motivated. Those who have done no wrong, have nothing to fear, has been Modi's consistent stand.

In all fairness, despite these unprecedented reforms leading to far greater tax compliance and effective monitoring, the parallel economy is still alive but is no longer thriving. With increased digital analytics and the use of AI by the tax administration, the ability of the taxman to 'track, connect and act' has dramatically improved. The linkage of Permanent Account Number (PAN), the Aadhar Card and the Income Tax Return has given a substantial boost to detecting undisclosed income or asset mismatches. AI based risk profiling has become a part of all scrutiny tax assessments. On the other hand, life has become easier for the commoner who has to pay no income-tax on an annual income up to ₹12.75 lakhs.

In 2025, even Modi's critics agree that extensive use of black money now prevails more only in certain sectors of the economy like real estate, iron and steel scrap, jewellery and some benami stock exchange transactions. Apart from such sectors, most businesses have concluded after a risk-reward analysis, that it makes little commercial sense to evade tax.

Evading taxes is not the only reason for generating cash. All illegal and illegitimate payments are necessarily cash transactions including payment of bribes, protection money, political funding including inducement to voters. Such payments do not carry a moral stigma in a society used to it for generations. During Modi's 11 years in power, for the first time a government has displayed the political will and implemented consistent measures to combat the problem.

In the long run, GST and Unified Payments Interface (UPI), coupled with AI driven advanced analytics, and with the tax authorities having access to 6.5 billion digital transaction data sets, will make the risk reward analysis of generating black money, enormously costly and difficult. However, like many Asian countries, the cash culture is so deeply rooted and endemic in India, that it cannot be uprooted easily even by the marathon efforts of Narendra Modi.

Black may yet not be ugly, but it is no longer beautiful.

CHAPTER TWELVE

Balance Sheet of the Mission

1

IN SEPTEMBER 2025, the Republic of India and Narendra Modi are both 75. Modi has held elective public office as the Chief Minister of Gujarat and then as Prime Minister of India for 24 years, without a break. In March 2026, Modi will surpass the record of Pawan Kumar Chamling Rai for holding elective public office in India for the longest time. Chamling was the Chief Minister of Sikkim from 1994 to 2019.

No family. No friends. No holidays. No vacations. No celebrations. A minimum 16-hour working day throughout the year. Modi has been a relentless, non-stop machine on 24/7, 365 days' national service for more than 24 years. Prior to that, 30 years as full time Sangh *pracharak* and BJP functionary, that is, a total of 54 years of public service. Modi shows not the slightest sign of fatigue or even slowing down. What is the source of his superhuman energy and what are the forces which motivate him.

What distinguishes Modi from most other politicians and leaders is his sheer genuineness. His objective has never been the pursuit of raw power. Even his worst detractors admit that Modi is motivated by service. Only after he became Gujarat chief minister, he realized how critical power was to render the most effective and highest level of service to the people.

Despite a string of successes, from making BJP win state and municipal elections to organizing nationwide movements for generating public awareness, for over 30 years, first as a *pracharak,* and then as a party functionary, Modi neither aimed for, nor occupied, any elective public office in Gujarat or elsewhere. As a disciplined soldier of the party, he underwent political exile imposed by senior leaders, until he was instructed by Vajpayee and Advani to take over the Chief Ministership of Gujarat almost overnight, when he was 51. In Indian legislative history, Modi is unique for becoming a chief minister as a first time MLA and becoming the Prime Minister as a first time MP.

As generations of bureaucrats have testified, Modi is a dazzlingly brilliant learner on the job. He listens; he is curious; he asks; he delves into the minutest detail; he follows up; he evaluates; he decides. If you are underprepared and sloppy, you will be jettisoned. He has zero patience for fools who steal his time.

As his confidence grew exponentially in his own ability to administer and deliver service, Modi had to strategically neutralize those obstructing his work or who were self seeking, venal or inferior administrators. He cannot be faulted, if some of the tactics he adopted in doing so, were borderline Machiavellian. No strong leader fails to radiate an aura of ruthlessness.

Modi believes in what Krishna preached to Arjun in the Gita. When Arjun is hesitant to fight with his cousins, teachers, and elders, Krishna reminds him that the war is not personal; it is to uphold righteousness or dharma. Modi has adopted this as the core philosophy of life. And there was no shortage of Duryodhanas in Gujarat.

Despite the handicap of his Ghanchi caste not being a dominant caste in highly caste conscious Gujarat, Narendra Modi consolidated his power in 2007, after handsomely winning the assembly elections for a second time, despite Keshubhai's public dissent. Modi was such a cut above the rest that he easily transcended complex caste equations.

2

September 2007 was the turning point when he intuitively felt that the Cosmic wanted him to demonstrate to the world that Gujarat was a model state which India would soon emulate. It is time you went to Delhi; Modi was urged by his closest supporters. This was not naked ambition; it was pure aspiration. And they had every reason to so believe.

The Gujarat Model under Narendra Modi (2001- 2014) was nothing short of an economic miracle. The state's economy grew at an average of 10% annually, as against

India's 6.5%. Its share of national industrial output rose to a dramatic 17%, contributing around 8% to India's GDP. Gujarat recorded an average of 8% annual agricultural GDP growth; more than double India's rate of 3.3%; surpassing even Punjab's Green Revolution era. By 2006, 95% of Gujarat villages had dedicated 24-hour rural electrification. 98.8% of villages were linked via *pucca* all-weather roads. By 2014, Gujarat maintained 74,000 kilometres of such roads. India's first 1 MW solar installation was launched on the Narmada Canal.

Development-focused; investment-friendly; streamlined single window clearance; businesslike and not bureaucratic approach; rapid infrastructure growth; impressive by world standards for developing countries. Global business schools vied with each other to study the Gujarat model.

Modi's operational style was of a CEO in a hurry; far removed from the anachronistic functioning of a half sleepy-eyed state CM. Gone were the days in Gujarat when the bureaucrats took all critical decisions, with the politics-obsessed ill-informed CM being barely aware. Modi corporatized the government. Meetings were intense crisp and structured. Participants came prepared to be quizzed by Modi. External experts were freely tapped. Modi's growing technical grasp stunned the officers. Seasoned entrepreneurs were awestruck with Modi's execution capabilities, considering that he was not dealing with smart MBAs from fancy business schools, rather generalist bureaucrats to whom modern management principles had so far been alien.

Every secretary and senior officer in the Gujarat

government was required by Modi to regularly visit at the Taluka and village level to assess and follow up on the progress of development initiatives and report to him in detail. Modi himself regularly visited villages, including having lunch with children in school, to firsthand evaluate the situation on the ground. Modi mastered micro details about the smallest village on the map of Gujarat. The phrase 'hands on' acquired a new meaning, recall Modi's close associates today, 'he even instructed us how to efficiently staple papers.'

In a country where dynastic succession has become the norm, Narendra Modi clinically severed all family ties. At 17, he left home, never to return. He spurned matrimony and broke the shackles of normality. He had no godfathers and no connections. He acquired the reputation for doing favours to none. This obviously meant sacrificing several strong relationships cultivated over the years in the Sangh and the party. If friends turned rivals had to be opposed in the larger interest of the mission, Modi showed no hesitation. This made the masses believe that their welfare was Modi's only concern.

In the laboratory of Gujarat, Modi began to understand the issues which India faced. However, during the first decade of the Millennium, Modi's entire focus was exclusively on his state. By 2007, development had already exorcised the ghosts of Godhra from the mind of most. Despite this, at the national level, he maintained a low profile and hardly participated in the 2004 and 2009 BJP Lok Sabha campaigns led by Advani.

It was only in 2011, when the Vibrant Gujarat Summit attracted international attention (delegations from 100 countries signed MOUs worth USD 320 billion for Gujarat), that Modi decided it was time to serve not only Gujarat. Ageing Advani had not succeeded on two successive occasions, and the BJP had no credible PM face to replace him. Pramod Mahajan, a strong probable for the role, had been shot dead by his brother in April 2006, over a family feud. The others were relative political lightweights. In 2011, Modi embarked on a fast for communal harmony and people saw a softer, youth friendly, tech savvy and moderate Hindutva image. His seamless transformation as a national leader had begun.

3

Despite the spotless personal integrity of Dr Manmohan Singh, the Congress led UPA coalition was being wrecked by scam after scam. Anti-corruption crusaders like Anna Hazare were embarrassing the government daily. Modi's belief grew firmer that he could do for India what he had done for Gujarat. His blood boiled at India's lack of response against growing Pakistan sponsored repeated terrorist attacks in Mumbai and elsewhere. Modi said in a recent interview about the Balakot Air Strike: 'I wanted to erase the shame of the 2008 Mumbai terror attacks when the military literally pleaded to be allowed to take decisive action against Pakistan but was denied by the political leadership.'

In 2012, he notched a third electoral victory in Gujarat with a growing share of the Muslim vote for the BJP. The Sangh decided to throw its full weight behind Narendra Modi. Many in the BJP had begun to realize that a third electoral failure would be disastrous. Destiny had deftly made Modi, the most obvious choice for his party cadres.

Modi was not wanting to be the Prime Minister of India for satisfying his personal ambition. His aspiration was to lead the nation to make it strong and vibrant. He genuinely believed that he was the optimal person to lead. This was not delusional thinking or megalomania, as events would later testify. He was seeking power so that he could implement his ideas and plans for the country. He had national pride, not personal ego. This is what made his candidature so instinctively appealing across the nation. Obstacles and individuals obstructing Modi's mission started falling apart one by one. Without any act or application on Modi's part.

At 85, Advani had to swallow the bitter truth that everyone cannot be Morarji Desai who had achieved his prime ministerial ambition at 81. Clever and capable leaders like Arun Jaitley shelved their own candidature and began to canvas for Modi. So did the firebrand Sushma Swaraj (who in 1999 had threatened to shave her head if the Italian origin Sonia became PM) after some initial hesitation. Rajnath Singh, then BJP president, spoken of in some circles as a possible aspirant himself, was vocal in supporting the appointment of Modi as head of BJP's Election Coordination Committee, the first step in Modi's coronation. Only those who had fancied their own slim chances, like Murli Manohar Joshi and Yashwant Sinha, opposed. With the Sangh and a million grassroots workers solidly behind Modi, such opposition was easily neutralized. The forces of destiny had chiselled a picture-perfect national entry.

Modi was a perfect foil to the Nehru-Gandhi dynasty. The Nehruvian offerings had begun to reek of staleness to the electorate. There was all round inertia and the UPA government was floundering. The aftermath of Bofors, 2G telecom scam, the Commonwealth games fraud, Coalgate and a string of corruption scandals had rocked the nation. Sonia Gandhi, after showing the sagacity to appoint PV Narasimha Rao (1991) and Dr Manmohan Singh (2004) as her nominee Prime Ministers, could have opted for the seasoned Pranab Mukherjee. However, she thought that her family was now mature enough to lead. Congress election posters began showing only one face. The BJP was not going to kick a gift horse in the mouth.

In contrast, Modi's administrative experience, stellar personal integrity, and thirteen years of squeaky-clean government in Gujarat, was highly attractive to the voters. '*Na khaoonga, na khaane doonga*' slogan of Modi worked wonders. Narendra Modi had no family, no children, no wealth, no vested interest. No dynasty to spawn and no Empire to create. He was a die hard maverick on a mission. And then, the inexperienced opposition on the other side, committed a political blunder by terming Modi a communalist, which only resulted in Modi garnering even more votes. In the 2007 Gujarat elections, it had blundered likewise by calling Modi rather ugly names, which had terribly backfired.

During Dr Manmohan Singh's tenure, there had been 25 major serious Pakistan sponsored, terrorist attacks on Indian soil.

2005: Delhi bombings—60 killed.

2006: Mumbai suburban train bombings—200 killed.
2007: Hyderabad twin blasts—40 killed.
2008: 26/11 Mumbai attacks by 10 Pakistani terrorists at multiple locations—166 killed; dubbed India's 9/11.
2010: German Bakery blast, Pune—17 killed.
2011: Mumbai bombings—26 killed.
2013: Hyderabad blast—17 killed.

Dr Manmohan Singh had zero appetite for war or retaliation. Despite such grave and repeated provocation by Pakistan, the UPA government took no action due to compulsions of coalition politics and Congress' flawed policy of not upsetting the minority community. Not realizing that the Indian Muslim was as much a victim of these attacks as any other Indian. This proved to be a major factor in the defeat of the UPA. Only Narendra Modi can protect India from such constant attacks and had the guts to retaliate, thought the average Indian.

Modi ran the best ever presidential style election campaign in India. The focus was unabashedly on him as the transformative developmental leader of proven calibre. A poor man's son who understood how the poor survived and what they felt. An ordinary tea vendor, who had dedicated his entire life to the country. People versus Privilege. 3D holograms of Modi at virtual rallies added to the mystic. His firebrand oratory reflected his confidence of victory. Prior to every election rally, there was immaculate homework and brainstorming by Team Modi, as to which topic would strike the greatest chord in the head and heart of the voter. His conversational, folksy, colourful style helped. He spewed fire and brimstone at Pakistan.

'Pakistan is sending terrorists into our country, and the government in Delhi is writing them love letters,' Modi thundered in his campaign speech at Jammu. 'India will not be seen with weak eyes anymore. We will talk to Pakistan in the language it understands', he said in Patna. UPA's strategic restraint will be replaced by Modi's muscular nationalism. Modi's style, of referring to himself in the third party, proved novel ('*is Modi ke Hathon se, kuch acche kaam honewale hai!*'— Some good national deeds will be undertaken by Modi, when he is Prime Minister). He often referred to the beheading of Indian soldiers by Pakistan and said that 'while Pakistan kills our soldiers, the Congress government gives them biryani'. Modi was referring to the warm hospitality shown by the UPA government to the visiting Pakistan delegation. 'India needs a government which puts national security above vote bank politics', he said. Emphasizing the need for India to encourage indigenous production of defence equipment and arms, he graphically said at a rally at the Mahalaxmi racecourse in Mumbai, 'when the bullets piercing the enemy's chest have been manufactured in India, that is a matter of national pride'. In Hindi, this sounded even better. Before the listeners left the rally, they had made up their mind to vote for Modi.

Those votes were multiplied manifold by the mastery of Amit Shah in executing the electoral arithmetic and understanding the dynamics of the Indian election scene from the smallest polling booth to the largest counting centre. Shah has psephology in his DNA.

More than anything else, there was an electricity in the air. Something was about to materially change. The jingle of '*Hum Modiji ko laanewale hai; aur achhé din aane walé hai*', (We are going to bring Modi. Good days are ahead!), was heard nationwide Even traditional Congress voters and non-BJP supporters realized that Narendra Modi had something unique to offer to the nation. No corruption. No nepotism. No dynasty. No cowardice. No nit-picking nonsense. Development. Technology. Speed. Efficiency. Hard work. A proven track record of impeccable service. Modi was the perfect commodity on offer to the Indian voters.

A section of the elite, electorally inconsequential, but nevertheless influential in opinion building, had little doubt about Modi's native intelligence, integrity, efficiency and dedication. However, for them, every outstanding quality of Modi was negated by his Hindutva credentials. The Nehruvian aversion towards so-called mixing religion with politics, was so deeply embedded in their mind that issues of probity in public life, national security, alleviation of poverty through rapid development, economic transformation, all became secondary to their obsession that the Prime Minister of India must have impeccable 'secular' credentials. He cannot be a Hindu nationalist.

History will record that Narendra Modi's election as Prime Minister uprooted this ideological obsession from India's national psyche. The elite's hitherto dominant role of the political dialogue has been relegated to a squeak in the back room. As it often happens, the pendulum has now swung to the other side, accelerated by a worldwide shift to the right. This is a structural, not a cyclical change. Hinduism has shed its indolence. And significantly, it is the youth which is the most charged up. It will be difficult to find a single future prime minister, in the decades to come, who does not believe in the idea of a civilizational cultural, non-theocratic, Hindu Rashtra.

All these years, secularism was misconstrued as negation or sterilization of history, appeasement of the minority, affirmative action in economic benefits and job reservations, feeble response to provocation from Pakistan, stifling political correctness and allergy to Hinduism as a way of life. The Indian political spectrum will no longer be divided on this issue. This transformational change in national thinking will be attributed to Narendra Modi.

4

On the other hand, Modi has been scrupulously even handed in his actions which affect the minorities. The cobwebs are being fast removed from the minds of Indian Muslims and Indian Christians, particularly women, about Narendra Modi. None can allege the slightest discrimination by India's Welfare State, which is religion neutral. Communal peace has been the norm under Modi, with not a single major or high-fatality communal conflagration. BJP's minority vote share is consequently registering gains across the country. Modi's personal popularity amongst Muslims is rising.

Modi has not committed a single constitutional impropriety. Unlike Indira Gandhi, the Modi government has never attempted to overrule any uncomfortable or unpalatable Court judgement by introducing a constitutional amendment. Even when the 99th Constitutional Amendment, which had the unanimous support of all political parties, was held to be invalid by the Supreme Court, Modi showed utmost respect for the Court and refused to re-introduce it. He has never obstructed judicial process or used intemperate language about the judiciary. And yet the party which declared the Emergency, suspended civil liberties and suppressed dissent, introduced press censorship, amended the Constitution when virtually the entire opposition was in jail, has the temerity to allege that Modi is undermining the Constitution.

The perennial struggle between successive governments and the Supreme Court over appointment of judges of the High Courts and the Supreme Court has not bothered Modi much. Unlike Indira Gandhi, he does not want a 'committed judiciary'. There have been instances in the recent past when Modi has personally intervened to ensure that a proposed appointee with domain knowledge and integrity is not prevented from becoming a judge on account of what is perceived to be his sociopolitical bias or predilection. At the end of the day, however, in a country where judicial review is endless, no government wants a persistently politically hostile judge. It is only a matter of time before a compromise solution emerges between the present Collegium system, and appointment of judges by the Executive.

However, what causes Modi personal anguish is the growing and consistent talk about corruption and nepotism in parts of the higher judiciary. A recent episode where unaccounted currency notes were found at the residence of a Delhi High Court judge during an operation to extinguish fire; and initiation of impeachment proceedings against him in Parliament, due to his steadfast refusal to resign, is one such instance. It is most dangerous when the common man comes to believe that there is lack of probity in the higher judiciary. A dramatic cleanup of the system is therefore a matter of time. If a committed judiciary is bad for democracy, a compromised judiciary is worse. If the salt has lost its savour, wherewith can it be salted.

During 11 years of his prime ministership so far, reforms initiated to remove legal and regulatory bottle- necks resulted in elimination of 40,000 unnecessary compliances and the statute book has been cleaned up with the repeal of 1500 redundant laws. The Lord Macaulay-authored Victorian-era Indian Penal Code, 1860, has been replaced with the Bharatiya Nyaya Samhita (Indian Justice Code), to accelerate the snailpaced criminal justice system. 288 minor offences are being decriminalized to spare harassment to those without legal resources.

5

During Modi's eleven years at the helm, India's global stature has been enhanced. Modi began his foreign affairs innings with a bang by inviting leaders of neighbouring countries, including Pakistan to his first swearing in ceremony. When it comes to foreign affairs, Narendra Modi is always ready to assimilate and absorb. Few know that before he became

Gujarat CM, he had crisscrossed almost every state in America on a Greyhound bus. He is on first name terms with the Indian diaspora in far flung countries like Mauritius, Guyana and Suriname. His knowledge about Nepal is encyclopaedic, acquired during his Kailash Mansarovar yatra and Himalayan sojourns.

Modi enthusiastically has introduced every innovative idea which he spotted abroad. The bullet train project in Maharashtra-Gujarat owes its origin to Modi being impressed by the clockwork precision of the Shinkansen, the Japanese bullet trains; the Berlin railway station inspired him to modernize railway stations at home; cleanup operations of a river in Seoul helped the operations to clean the Ganga; the Prime Minister's Affordable Housing Scheme was inspired by what Modi admired in public housing provided by Singapore. Reciprocally, he has enhanced India's reputation as a reliable development partner by undertaking successful projects like the Metro rail and the Supreme Court building in Mauritius, post-earthquake rehabilitation in Nepal, modern ambulance service in Sri Lanka or the Vaccine Diplomacy during COVID-19.

The Vaccine diplomacy, by India emerging as the world's largest vaccine manufacturer, and supplying 301 million doses to other countries, generated immense international goodwill. Modi leveraged India's goodwill to successfully mount large-scale evacuation operations to rescue stranded Indians from war zones and disaster-affected areas across the world. In 2015, during the Yemen Civil War when the Houthi rebels captured Sana'a, the Indian Navy and Air Force launched

Operation Rahat rescuing 4,741 Indians along with nearly 300 foreign nationals. That same year, under Operation Maitri, India conducted massive relief and evacuation efforts following the devastating Nepal earthquake, bringing home around 3,900 Indians. In 2016, under Operation Sankat Mochan, 153 Indians and 2 Nepalis were airlifted from conflict-ridden South Sudan. In 2018, the Navy's Operation Nistar evacuated 38 Indians stranded on Socotra Island, Yemen, after Cyclone Mekunu.

When the world was struck by COVID-19, India mounted the unprecedented Vande Bharat Mission and Operation Samudra Setu, repatriating more than 9.2 million Indians from 72 countries—an exercise unparalleled in scale and efficiency. In 2021, during the Taliban takeover of Afghanistan, over 1,000 Indians and Afghan minorities were rescued under Operation Devi Shakti in extremely perilous conditions. In 2022, under Operation Ganga, India evacuated more than 22,500 Indians, mostly students, from war-torn Ukraine. In 2023, Operation Kaveri brought back nearly 4,000 Indians during the Sudan Civil War, while Operation Ajay facilitated the evacuation of over 1,300 Indians from Israel amid the conflict.

Each of these operations, without exception, was personally supervised by Modi. Not even the United States or Russia could have matched what India achieved. Together, these missions stand as compelling evidence of Modi's stature and credibility as a true global leader.

Having regard to the geopolitical situation, Narendra Modi has always been extremely keen to ensure that India's reliance on fossil fuels ends, which makes him an ardent supporter of renewables and biofuels, like the direction for mandatory 20% to 27% blending of ethanol into petrol, and soon possibly diesel, as also solar power, in which Gujarat showed the way to India. Wind power, flex car engine with 85% ethanol, hydrogen, are areas where rapid progress is seen. In 2014, solar PV module manufacturing capacity was 2.5 GW, which reached 100 GW in 2025.

India achieved its target of 50% electric power from non-fossil fuels in 2025, five years ahead of the targeted date. India's petroleum minister has recently talked about a huge potential oil reserve in the Andaman Islands up to nearly 184,440 crores litres, which will obviously be a game changer. A National Deepwater Exploration Mission to harness ocean energy has been embarked upon. Modi has been acutely conscious of the connection between oil dependence and India's national security. Only he could have managed the fine balance of warmth with both Israel and the Middle East which India enjoys.

Modi never tires emphasizing about India becoming self-reliant in its energy and fertilizer requirements. He believes that the transformative fiscal savings (USD 47 billion every year in the short term; collective estimated savings of USD 262 billion upto 2047) can expedite his dream of a Viksit Bharat much earlier than the planned 2047 the centenary of Bharat's Independence.

Successive foreign secretaries and foreign ministers have testified to Modi's micromanagement of external affairs with real problem-solving exercises and detailed scenario planning enacted regularly in the Prime Minister's office. Modi's foreign visits are notorious for their punishing schedule. The man does not sleep and does not let anyone in his team sleep. Whether it involves an increase in the Haj quota for Indian Muslims or the construction of a grand Swaminarayan Hindu Temple in Abu Dhabi or reducing energy costs in Qatar, are all attributable to Modi's personal equation with the Rulers of the Gulf countries. The UAE treats Modi as a reliable friend in a crisis and has reciprocated accordingly. Modi has remained friendly with both Zelenskyy and Putin; with Iran and Israel. With a single warm hug, Modi seems to mesmerize most.

6

During 11 years of Narendra Modi's Prime Ministership, India's economic progress has been spectacular. Nominal GDP climbed from USD 2.03 trillion to 4.3 trillion. From tenth rank in nominal World GDP, India moved to fourth. This makes India the fastest growing large economy, targeting a GDP of USD 5 trillion by March 2028. As far as infrastructure is concerned, 99% rural road connectivity was achieved and national highways increased from 91,000 kilometres to 145,000 kilometres; optical fibre to village panchayats from 59,000 kilometres to 214,000; 74 operational airports increased to 160, connecting 88 new destinations; and metro rail coverage jumped from 248 kilometres to 1013 kilometres. With the allocation of money on the Railways increasing 9 times since 2014, 136 world class Vande Bharat trains showcase India's pride, which are planned to reach 400 soon.

The long-stalled (nearly 25 years) Vadhavan all-weather Port project in Maharashtra (will be India's largest; 10th in the world) was revived by Modi's personal intervention. FDI inflows have been the highest ever in Indian history at over USD 81 billion (FY 24-25). In 2014, persons below the poverty line were 29.1% of the population, which stands reduced to 13%. Direct Benefit Transfer (DBT) of welfare benefits increased from 0.06 lakh crores to a staggering 43 lakh crores cumulatively. Digital and financial inclusion has increased by leaps and bounds. Jan Dhan bank accounts from 1.5 Crores to 56 Crores. Nearly every village in India has access to a bank now. UPI has the amazing unparalleled-in-the- world ability to process 640 million daily transactions, and Internet users rose from 25 crores to 90 crores. No wonder that India leads the world in real-time digital payments. Forex reserves increased from USD 304 billion to USD 700 billion, while inflation halved from 9.4% to 4.8%. Fiscal deficit is down to 4.4%. This has been achieved, despite disruptive major structural reforms like introduction of GST, the new Bankruptcy Code, and labour code rationalisation; as also the slowdown during COVID-19.

7

Narendra Modi just delivered his 12th consecutive Independence Day Speech as Prime Minister from the ramparts of the Red Fort. Modi's Mission has unfolded so consistently and seamlessly between his first (2014) and his latest (2025) Independence Day speech. It is a tale of promises not only kept but far exceeded.

In 2014, the Prime Minister had called for a national movement to 'Make in India' ('come, make in India. Sell anywhere but make here'). Eleven years later, this movement has evolved into the concept of Atmanirbhar (Self-reliant) which Modi emphasized in his latest address. The concept has concretized into the National Manufacturing Mission to build 5G infrastructure indigenously with the target of USD 7.5 trillion manufacturing GDP by 2047.

It is difficult to believe that a proposal to manufacture semiconductors in India gathered dust for more than half a century until Modi's government revived it. A semiconductor pioneer, Robert Noyce's proposal to set up a plant in 1964 was shelved by the Congress government, which made Noyce establish Intel Corp. in Hong Kong. Today, under Modi, six semiconductor units are in different stages of execution, and four more have been approved. This is a classic instance of the 'License Raj' contrasted with Modi's rapid implementation of whatever he conceives. In his 2025 address, Modi said that India will manufacture its first indigenously developed chip before 2026. This is critical for India's strides into AI, which requires huge compute power. He also mentioned about India manufacturing fighter Jet engines.

The Jan Dhan Yojana announced in his 2014 address was launched within 13 days, with 1.5 crores accounts opened on Day One, which, 11 years later, have increased to more than 56 crores accounts. This was the foundation stone of

Modi's 'JAM Trinity' (Jan Dhan bank accounts, Aadhaar Card and mobile phone) for facilitating Direct Benefit Transfer of welfare benefits to the underserved citizens.

Modi had announced in his first address about creating separate toilets for girls and the Swachh Bharat Abhiyan (which was launched within seven weeks of his 2014 address, on Gandhi's birthday). In 2025, the target of more than 12 crores toilets, including separate ones for girls, has already been achieved. Rural sanitation coverage rose from 39%, to 100% in 2019, with 600,000 villages declared 'Open Defecation Free'.

In 2014, Modi's vision for the country was nation building through cleanliness and sanitation, governance reforms and manufacturing in India. In 2025, Modi's government is speeding like a bullet train with big budgets and speedy implementation. Semiconductors, jet engines, air and missile defence shield, indigenously made weapons,10 more nuclear reactors. Skill India announced in 2014 is now in 2025, the highly financed Rs. 100,000 crore Pradhan Mantri Viksit Bharat Rojgar Yojana or the Youth Employment Scheme to generate 3.5 crores jobs, with specifically designed fiscal incentives.

In 2025, Modi has every right to be legitimately proud of his government's milestones. The ambitiousness of his tone is infectious. In a span of little over a decade, Modi resonates like the leader of an emerging superpower, not merely an efficient large developing country.

In 2014 at Modi's swearing in ceremony, Nawaz Sharif, Pakistan's Prime Minister, was in the audience as an honoured guest. In 2025, in Modi's Independence Day address, the jingoistic Munir has been called a nuclear blackmailer who will 'soon lose sleep'. Passive deterrence and calibrated response are now replaced with a clear warning that India treats both terrorists and their sponsors on the same footing as enemies of the State, to be dealt with in the same manner. And this is not empty rhetoric. The disgraceful Indus Valley Treaty has been suspended with the chilling warning that no water can flow alongside blood. The nervousness of the enemy is palpable.

Plans are afoot to launch India's modular space station. More than 300 space start-ups constitute a vibrant competitive private eco-system which is growing exponentially for which the Indian government has approved funds of more than ₹10 billion. In 35 years (1979 to 2014), 42 Indian Space Missions were launched. During Modi's 11 years, 60 missions were launched.

Between Modi's first and latest Independence Day speech, 25 crores Indians have been lifted out of poverty. Significantly, Naxal affected (left-wing extremism), districts which were 125 in 2014 dramatically stand reduced to just 18, which is attributable to the Naxals fast losing support of the local population.

A National Critical Minerals Strategy is in place, with more than 1200 plus exploration sites identified, as India embarks upon a journey towards minerals sovereignty, with the aspiration to emerge as a leader in critical mineral supply chains globally. The Prime Minister strongly stressed self-reliance in critical minerals in his 2025 speech.

While so far 1.7 million households have installed roof top solar systems, this is expected to reach 4 million by March 2026. Under this scheme, households receive free electricity up to 300 units and direct financial assistance for installation of the system. This move will revolutionize India's power sector and help in achieving its target of 500 GW of renewable energy by 2030.

Not unexpectedly, Standard & Poor's (S&P), after 18 long years, has upgraded India's long-term sovereign credit rating to BBB from BBB-(BBB minus).

8

Although Narendra showed clinical detachment in cutting ties with his family, his love and adoration for his mother remained constant. She was learned without being educated, he fondly remembers. He has always beheld the face of his mother in every image of the Divine Mother he has worshipped lifelong. His heart has been wrenched by the extremely hard life and suffering of his mother, and millions of women like her in India. He desperately wants to make them happy. Who knows better their embarrassment suffering humiliation and agony. This has made him obsessive about women welfare.

Ultimate happiness for Narendra Modi has been wiping the tear from every poor woman's eye and bringing a smile back on the face of every girl child in the country. From separate girls' toilets to free cooking gas cylinders, to direct transfer of money in her bank account, to screening rural women for cancer, to making safe pregnancy a mass movement (financial assistance provided to 3.98 crore pregnant women, with 6 crore free ante-natal check-ups), to grant women permanent commission in all branches of the armed forces, to elevating more women judges to the Supreme Court, to providing tap water at home, to eliminating female foeticide, to training women as agricultural drone pilots, to already creating 2 crores, out of the planned 3 crores, *Lakhpati Didis* (women having annual income of at least Rs. 100,000), to increasing maternity leave from 12 weeks to 26 weeks, to opening Sainik schools for women, to the increase in girl students in IIT's from 8% to 26%; to constantly messaging gender equality.

Narendra Modi successfully managed to secure all round political support for a revolutionary constitutional amendment in 2023 mandating 1/3rd (33%) reservation of seats for women in the Lok Sabha and all state legislative assemblies. This laudatory change will be implemented after completion of the National Census and consequent delimitation exercise. Presently, only 14% of Indian Parliamentarians are women.

Women, both Hindu and Muslim, have reciprocated their love for the PM. Criminalizing triple *talaq* has thrilled the latter. The blessings of millions of women is a powerful amulet of protection for Narendra Modi. Nothing pleases the Divine Mother more than a man who considers a woman superior to him.

9

Modi is a public health obsessive. Seasoned health-care professionals, both Indian and foreign, are stunned by his mastery of intricate details and the domain knowledge about vaccines he has acquired on the job. History will record that this is what saved India from an existential threat during the global COVID-19 crisis. Narendra Modi excelled himself during this crisis. The Prime Minister himself is truly proud of this achievement.

From the time the first whispers from Wuhan about the deadly virus, began to circulate, Modi put into place the whole of government approach. Some of his closest colleagues, at that stage, felt that he was overreacting. However, in his daily meditation, Modi increasingly felt that the coming crisis, if not tackled, would be an unmitigated disaster for India.

The first step was creating national awareness. His near spiritual connect with the Indian masses helped. The Great Communicator that he is, with a single superb public address, Modi embedded the issue into the national consciousness overnight. 'If we do not maintain discipline for 20 days, he said, India can go back by 20 years.' The chilling message touched every Indian citizen who instinctively realize that Modi was not speaking as the Prime Minister, but as a father of the family. The initial lockdown of 21 days, extended to 68 later, for a humongous country like India with all its attendant problems, was nothing short of a miracle.

Millions of citizens across the country, headed Modi's clarion call to thank the COVID-19 'healthcare warriors' who were risking their lives to save the country, by coming out on the balconies, to ring bells and thali at the given minute, as a symbolic gesture of national unity, which brought tears to many a hardened eye. With people power behind him, Narendra Modi swung into action.

The world's largest and most cost-effective vaccination exercise resulted in an infection to mortality ratio or Case Fatality Rate (CFR) which was the lowest in the world, barring small countries like Norway and Singapore. India's GDP per capita was 1/20th of Norway and 1/10th of Singapore. The structural challenges facing India on this front were known to Modi. With a population of 1.4 billion, the world's largest and terribly under-funded healthcare infrastructure (0.8 doctors per 1,000 people as compared to 4.5 doctors in Norway), inaccessible rural areas, illiteracy, multiple languages, and cultural-religious divides. Narendra Modi was not daunted by the magnitude of such challenges.

India administered 2.2 billion doses of the vaccine to 1 billion people, with every dose digitally tracked on the CoWin platform. Vaccines like Covishield and Covaxin were locally manufactured in a record time on a huge scale. Door-to-door drives, in tribal and rural areas with mass communication to convince and convert vaccine skeptics, were launched. To imagine the sheer scale of this exercise: Norway vaccinated 5 million and Singapore vaccinated 6 million, while India vaccinated over 1 billion people, often with limited cold-chain infrastructure and rural health workers. Given the conditions and density of India's population, air pollution, poverty, and crowded urban living; achieving a CFR better than the USA, UK, and Brazil was nothing short of a miracle. Modi's Covid-19 campaign will be recorded by history as the most effective large-scale mobilization of human and institutional efforts in modern public healthcare. Half of the vaccines in the world are now manufactured in India.

Modi decided personally on the timing of the declaration of the lockdown, which turned out to be technically perfect. He attributes this to intuition. Other countries like the United Kingdom suffered terribly by postponing it. While monitoring the situation and the nationwide vaccine drive on a 24/7 basis, Modi had to simultaneously address the issue of how to sustain the poor and underprivileged during the lockdown, particularly those who depended on daily wages or daily income, as also to keep the supply chains for essential items like milk and medicines running during the lockdown.

Modi mentions that during the crisis, many economists advised him to introduce free doles and cash distribution on a national scale. However, Modi points out that he did not implement their advice and managed the crisis without any such excessive public expenditure. The only concession on humanitarian grounds was providing ₹500/- in cash to nearly 20 crores women in extreme distress to tide over the lockdown.

From incentivizing the private sector to produce PPE overalls and N95 masks to ventilators; mobilizing the armed forces to transport oxygen tankers; transporting medical oxygen being required across the country during the second phase of the Pandemic; starting makeshift facilities and field hospitals; innovatively converting 4000 railway coaches into Covid facilities; providing free life insurance for 2 million health workers; there was no task which Modi did not personally overlook. Developed countries began to seek India's advice; and India, from experiencing a severe shortage, became an exporter of N95 masks.

Modi's personal office became a War Room during the crisis from where he coordinated daily with the state chief ministers, the armed forces, ministries like railways, textiles, and industry, expert healthcare professionals and the different vaccine manufacturers. The minutest detail bore Modi's imprimatur.

Millions of lives were saved and damage to the Indian economy minimized. One shudders to think what would have happened had there been any of the earlier Prime Ministers instead of Modi. Every crisis raises consciousness. COVID-19 transformed mind- sets in the ecosystem of Indian healthcare. The Prime Minister continues to maintain a vigil in frequent meetings against any future pandemic, keeping himself abreast of the latest medical developments.

Under Modi's Ayushman Bharat Scheme, 79 crores Indians have health accounts, and 9.50 crores health insurance cards have been issued. Six crores children and more than 1.50 crores pregnant women have been vaccinated, free of cost, against 12 infectious and other diseases. 5 crores economically handicapped Indians received free hospital admission. The Prime Minister-inspired innovative e-Sanjeevani tele-medical platform provides specialist health care to rural and remote areas of the country. So far, 34 crores Indians have been served.

Amrit Pharmacies provide affordable critical medicines to the deserving through Jan Aushadhi (medicine) Kendras. Citizens have saved ₹130,000 crores over the past decade due to this initiative. During Modi's Prime Ministership, the number of sophisticated All-India Institute of Medical

Sciences have increased to 23, and 1700 (including 780 MBBS) Medical Colleges are operational.

10

Despite zero technological or educational training, Modi's grasp of using technology across sectors, is intuitive. Modi feels satisfied in how he has mastered the art of applying technology to any given situation, which stuns technical experts. His team talks about his '*adbhut kshamta*' (amazing competence) in grasping scientific and technical facts.

Two decades ago, in 2003, as Gujarat CM, Modi had established an online grievance redressal system for the people, which received an UN award for improving transparency and accountability in public service. As Prime Minister, Modi launched a similar initiative called PRAGATI for monitoring national projects (363 projects reviewed so far) for removing bottlenecks and accelerating their execution. In 2010, under Modi's chief ministership, each of the 14,000 village Panchayats in Gujarat had broadband connectivity. He made Gujarat the first state to apply satellite geographic information systems to plan, implement and monitor watershed management. In 2025, 214,300 village Panchayats in rural India had universal digital access and the use of optical fibre broadband connectivity. As in Gujarat, so in India, and on a much grander scale.

Like approximately 83% of Indians today, Narendra's entire education was in the vernacular medium. He has therefore been extremely keen to ensure that those not proficient in English are not at a disadvantage. Bhashini, a government endeavour, provides AI-powered translation across Indian languages which assists business, government and startups to build vernacular tech solutions. The Prime Minister personally monitors this pet project of simultaneous AI-powered translation of parliamentary proceedings and debates in real time for users of nine languages including Tamil, Telugu, Marathi, Bengali and Gujarati, to begin with. India AI mission, a five-year programme launched by Modi in 2024, catalyses AI tools across Indian languages. It has a budget of USD 1.2 billion over five years. Those who have schooled in the vernacular are more aligned to a nationalist agenda. Providing them with a level playing field also makes eminent political sense.

In June 2025, the government began issuing e-passports with embedded chips to enhance security and comply with global standards. 1275 railway stations, from where Narendra's journey in life began, are being technically upgraded including Wi-Fi and digital signage. National Quantum Mission, a ₹6000 crores initiative launched in April 2023, supports technology hubs at the IITs for quantum computing. While the National Broadband Mission will extend optic fibre broadband connectivity to 270,000 villages with 5G/6G planning. A ₹20,000 Crores Research and Innovation Fund has been allocated for private sector R&D. During his tenure, 390 new Universities, and 7 new Indian Institute of Technology (IITs) were set-up. More than 1.6 crore youth were trained to acquire vocational skill sets.

Each of these technology initiatives were studied, approved

and are regularly monitored by Modi, with a near childlike fascination.

11

Prime Minister Rajiv Gandhi had frankly admitted in 1986, that citizens were only receiving 15 paise of every rupee of welfare benefit which the government was transferring to them. The balance 85% was eaten up by middlemen and lost on account of corruption and leakages. The 'Modi Quartet' (Jan Dhan bank account, Aadhaar card, mobile phone and the system of Direct Benefit Transfer) also called JAM Trinity, has revolutionalized the Indian Welfare State. Essentially, the idea is that every Indian citizen should have a bank account linked with his Aadhar Card and mobile phone enabling Direct Benefits Transfer (DBT) to be received straight into her bank account. Modi has made financial inclusion of the poorest, a national mission. Aadhar enables one to open a bank account in which one receives welfare benefits and other payments resulting in savings and enables access to insurance and other core financial products and services. Today 49 crores Indians, and 6.5 crores Indian merchants, use UPI, making it the world's envy.

According to the World Bank, 89% of Indians have a financial account of some kind, compared with only 35% in 2011. SEBI (stock market regulator) records reveal that more than 230 million have investment accounts, up nearly fivefold in last 5 years, and expected to reach 400 million by 2030. Indian stock markets raised a record USD 70 billion of equity finance (USD 19 billion in IPOs) in 2024—second only to the United States.

When it comes to adopting welfare initiatives begun by another government, Modi has never tried to politicize the issue. The classic example is the world- wide recognition of the success of Aadhar, a much- copied reliable biometric identity proof for every Indian resident. Nandan Nilekani, the father of the Aadhar experiment, has testified in the most glowing terms that despite Nilekani being the losing candidate in the 2014 elections on behalf of the Congress, Modi embraced the idea of Aadhar card warmly, and regularly sought Nilekani's advice.

12

Narendra Modi will be credited for launching the most scientific and systematic onslaught on poverty through development and an enhanced Welfare State, on a scale hitherto unknown in India.

Free electricity lights up the homes and smiles of lakhs of poor Indians. 3.6 crores urban and rural houses have so far been delivered under the Prime Minister's Awas Yojana, with 73% beneficiaries of this scheme, being women. Tap water is not far behind. 15 crores tap water connections (Har Ghar Jal) have already been provided to homes, where earlier women had to trudge far to fetch a pot of water.

The Prime Minister Garib Kalyan Anna Scheme provides five kilos of free food grains per person per month, to a staggering 81 crores Indians. Narendra Modi is personally aware what not having a toilet means. 12 crores new toilets have been provided so far to grateful women—particularly, schoolgirls who were prevented from attending school during menstruation.

Farmers have been a special part of Modi's Mission. The Prime Minister's Kisan Yojana is a flagship income support scheme for farmers. A 100% centrally funded scheme, it provides direct transfer of ₹6000/- per year to all landholding farmer families. 1.8 lakh Kisan (farmer) centres provide 'one stop shop' facility to farmers. To improve crop productivity, 25 crore Soil Health Cards have been distributed and an ambitious program for high-yielding seeds launched. Leading fertilizer companies have been encouraged to enter into farmer-partnerships where custom-made fertilizers are created to cater to specific weather conditions and to maximize yields. Solar pumps for farmers have multiplied during these 11 years at a growth of 44 times. 1500 Mandis (where farmers collectively sell products) have been linked via eNAM to dramatically improve market access. 142 crores saplings have been planted under the '*ek ped, ma ke naam*' campaign. India is now a proud world No. 1 for milk production. No. 2 in eggs and fish; and No. 5 in meat.

Modi can rightfully assert that he has given not just slogans but genuine development to the poor.

13

The Balance Sheet of Modi's Mission makes spectacular reading. To call him the best Prime Minister India ever had is an understatement. The fundamental changes in this decade

(2014-2025) in the Economy, Science and Technology and the Welfare State, are unparalleled. Rapid and calibrated response to the four terrorist attacks in these 11 years (as compared to 25 major terrorist episodes, which were unresponded, during Dr Singh's tenure) without involving the country in a long drawn-out war; no serious rioting and peaceful co-existence; the world's most effective management of the COVID-19 Pandemic.

Not even his worst critic will disagree that Modi is the most hard-working world leader with a hands-on approach and an eye for every minute detail in every single area. His ability to flit from subject to subject during his 16-hour day, for the last 24 years in public office, cannot be explained in rational terms alone.

'Discipline is in my DNA', he says. The clockwork precision of his day from dawn to dusk, supports the thesis of this book that his mind and body are instruments of a High Energy which constantly permeates him.

'Happy is the Kingdom whose subjects pray for the long life of their King, just as a father is loved by his sons', says Chanakya in *Arthashastra* of Kautilya. In Chapter 68 (Shanti Parva) of the *Mahabharata*, Bhishma similarly tells Yudhishthira, that 'a righteous King wins the love of his people; and the people pray for his long life'.

The effusive love of his people energizes Narendra Modi making him look daisy fresh at 8.30 p.m. after a gruelling day begun at 4 a.m., during which he has flown in and out of Delhi and participated in a dozen meetings. And this has been going on for the last 24 years without a single break.

Modi genuinely detests the language of majority-minority. There is growing realisation amongst people that there is no inconsistency between a State, which treats all its citizens and religions equally, and a civilisational, cultural Hindu Rashtra. Performance of the government has become the sole criteria of garnering votes. Caste community religion are being fast transcended. The tone and tenor of the political dialogue in the coming years will make all those who rely upon vote-bank politics, even more irrelevant than they already are today.

Imagine those underprivileged millions who are enjoying for the first time in their lives, the happiness of having cooking gas, a toilet, tap water, electricity, access to hospitals and medicines, free food grains, and money directly into the account of the housewife. Hindus, Muslims or Christians—they uniformly bless Narendra Modi personally, for what seems like, sudden light in their lives after decades of darkness and gloom. Their silent blessings are the cloak of protection over Modi's head.

Narendra Modi will become iconic in the next few decades. As India becomes a Superpower, a hundred years after Independence, the Nation will gratefully acknowledge both the Mahatma for 1947, and Modi for 2047. The Prime Ministers who will follow him, irrespective of party affiliation, will endeavour to emulate him. For all will be evaluated against Narendra Modi's yardstick.

Epilogue

The Sacrifice

1

A POOR CHILD WITH five siblings in a small town without electricity having barely enough to eat; receives substandard education in the vernacular; without access to radio television or newspapers; sacrifices his youth, abandons home in spiritual pursuit at 17; spurns matrimony and severs family ties; has zero political connections. Becomes Chief Minister of a large Indian state and is elected thrice to remain in office for 13 years, which state he transforms into a World Bank endorsed model state. Is elected as Prime Minister of India for three successive terms during which period India becomes the fastest growing large economy in the world having the largest volume of both digital payments and broadband users in the world; is top ranked globally in biometric identity systems, generic drug supply and public health coverage. It also becomes the largest internet connected democracy and the largest rural optic fibre network. He launches the world's most successful vaccination drive and saves millions of lives not only in India but in 97 other countries.

Narendra Modi has pulled crores out of poverty and revolutionized the welfare of women in the country. He has given the latter dignity, financial independence, and accelerated the movement towards gender equality. He has defended the borders of his motherland firmly, without being jingoistic, against a nuclear armed neighbour, who borders on being a rogue State. India has gained global stature as never before, and he has emerged as a global statesman. From generals to soldiers, the armed forces adore him. He has attracted the highest foreign investment in Indian history. During his prime ministership, India has become the fourth largest stock market globally with a total market capitalisation in excess of USD 5 trillion.

He has never been accused of corruption or nepotism, even by his worst enemies. Public officials revere and respect him for his superhuman hard work, dedication, and eye for detail. He is worshipped by his party cadres.

It has been conclusively established by independent Commissions of Enquiry, the SIT and the Supreme Court of India that the Godhra train burning incident, which took place in the first 20 weeks of his ever holding a public office, was a pre-meditated attack. The SIT concluded, and the Supreme Court upheld SIT's findings, that Modi was in no manner complicit or responsible for the communal violence which followed. Left leaning historians, Western media and a section of India's intellectual elite, deliberately and dishonestly continue to blank out Modi's public and repeated judicial exoneration.

Modi has not forgotten the Sangh's and BJP's agenda of India being a civilizational cultural *Hindu Rashtra*. He has never advocated though a theocratic state or even a non-theocratic state with an official religion. He has ended Kashmir's special constitutional status, which was wholly inconsistent with India's stand that Kashmir is an integral part of the country. For 72 long years, no other Indian prime minister could do this. Similarly, he ensured the construction of the Ram Mandir at the disputed Ayodhya site and ended 134 years of litigation and violence.

During his 11 years so far as Prime Minister Narendra Modi has changed the mindset of the people who are beginning to see India with pride and self-respect. He is perceived by more than 1 billion people including those who don't vote for him, as a national leader, transcending party lines and politics. The common man requires no statistics to know as to how every facet of his daily life has improved. India feels safe on its borders, and the Indian feels safer on the street.

And all this has been achieved within the democratic and constitutional framework. Elections are held fairly and transparently. Opposition parties (non-BJP) freely rule 31% of the states and union territories. Nobody is arrested for the most vitriolic trolling and caricaturing of Modi. Newspapers printed or digital, which are wired to criticize him, continue to be published. Narendra Modi has not declared any Emergency or suspended civil liberties or put opposition leaders in jail or imposed press censorship. The higher judiciary remains independent and continues to give many decisions against the government.

2

Even those who adore or admire Narendra Modi, do not realize the extent of his sacrifice. As a child of nine years, Narendra would instinctively realize that even though he still felt hungry, he should not help himself to another roti or ask for two more spoons of *dal*, for if he did so, his mother who ate the leftovers after everyone had finished, would go to bed on an empty stomach. And this did not happen once in a blue moon, it happened regularly.

Narendra's innate sensitivity and compassion for the helpless and his motivation to serve was present from an early age. He says that he received *seva na sanskaar* (service as an instilled cultural value) from his mother. The Tapti River often overflowed during a cloudburst causing heavy floods in Surat. While in High School, Narendra set up stalls to sell home made food, in a mela, and donated the sale proceeds, however small, to the flood affected people. He also worked a lot in the tribal belt.

Some children never have a childhood. Narendra was one of them. His childhood photographs show a contemplative, slightly sad expression. What went on in that large head, which made him join the Sangh at eight, no one knows. His father was dead against it. Narendra has never forgotten what he learnt in the Sangh starting with the Somnath temple.

Modi takes his trusteeship of the Somnath temple extremely seriously and devotes considerable time to it. He dreams of a gorgeously revamped Somnath becoming India's Vatican.

If a survival mode childhood toughened him, teenage was more spartan and in an active service mode. He was excited serving tea to the soldiers travelling to Delhi during the two wars. Narendra was different from his siblings and friends. His youthful energy was expended in Sangh activities and in swimming, cooking and washing clothes for the family, and obsessively visiting the many temples in Vadnagar. Yet he was an extrovert. He was an undisputed leader and troublemaker in school. He bombarded his elders and teachers with the usual questions of an intelligent child—'Why' and 'Why not?' He loved people but was not attached to them with the solitary exception of his mother. Even after Modi became Prime Minister, she visited him only once and continued to stay with his younger brother in a middle-class household in Gujarat.

3

For those who can discern, underneath Narendra Modi's tough looking persona, lies a sensitive and perceptive individual. From childhood, he has felt spiritually hungry and continues to do so. His heart is filled with reverence for many a spiritually advanced soul, he has encountered over more than six decades, and who cleared his doubts and questions. Yet he does not like to identify himself as a disciple of any one particular saint or Guru.

When Narendra, inspired by Vivekananda, was keen to join the Ramakrishna Mission as a monk, Swami Atmasthananda categorically told him that his path to spirituality was not to be a monk but through active service of the people. Later in 2007, when Modi was Gujarat Chief Minister, the Swami was elected as the 15th President of the Mission and occupied a place of deep reverence in Modi's heart, who called him his 'guiding light'.

Narendra received an identical message from Pramukh Swami Maharaj, head of the Swaminarayan movement. When Modi was 31, he met the Maharaj, on the banks of the Sabarmati river in Ahmedabad, who was blessed with great spiritual powers, including *vaaksiddhi*, and who told Modi, 'Our feet share the same lines', a profoundly significant prediction that Modi's entire life will be dedicated to service. Modi often sought spiritual solace from him until the latter's demise at a very advanced age. A reason why possibly Pakistan's ISI selected Akshardham, the headquarters of the Swaminarayan movement in Gujarat, for a terrorist attack, in September 2002. Evidence to what extent the rogue State can go.

Though many believe that Swami Dayanand of Rishikesh was Modi's spiritual Master or Guru, the Swami, a civil engineer until he took sanyaas, himself asserted that he was 'only a teacher, not a Guru'. Modi revered him as a practical saint who lived for others.

Another spiritual personage who had a profound effect on Modi was Swami Iswarananda Giri of Mount Abu in Rajasthan. In 2007, when Modi was Gujarat Chief Minister, at a huge religious gathering, whose video recording went viral, the Swami smiled and addressed Modi as Prime Minister. Upon Modi instantly correcting him, the Swami laughed and asserted that he had made no mistake. The saint followed the tradition of Kriya Yoga taught by Lahiri Mahasaya, Yukteshwara Giri, and Paramhansa Yogananda, whose lineage extends to Mahavatar Babaji himself. Kriya Yoga is an integral part of Modi's daily morning sadhana.

Modi has great regard for other saints and spiritual leaders across sects. The 'Hugging Saint'—Amritanandamayi, born in a small fishing village in Kerala; Swami Chinmayananda Saraswati, founder of the Chinmaya Mission for spread of Advait Vedanta, who spearheaded a global Hindu spiritual cultural resurgence; and Swami Chidananda Saraswati of Rishikesh; have all significantly uplifted Narendra Modi's consciousness.

Although a Shaiv and Vaishnav bhakta, and a lifelong Shakti and Ganesh upaasak, Modi has had a strong affinity for the Buddha, whose gorgeous bust regally surveys the Prime Minister's office. Modi's deep reverence for the Buddha is well known.

Every spiritual realisation—*Adhyaatmic Anubhuti*—is unique, believes Narendra Modi, like a person who plunges into the waters of Ganga, has a different direct experience, every single time that he does so.

Modi has no hesitation at all in stating that he has always enjoyed divine protection or spiritual guidance from the Cosmic. He firmly believes that so long as he feels connected with the Cosmic Energy, there is never a feeling of loneliness.

4

A dispassionate look at the 75 years of Narendra Modi reveals how every major incident and event in his life was structured in a manner to ensure the ultimate result. Many of us are children of destiny but some like Modi and Gandhi are instruments of the forces which shape India's emergence as a Nation.

Serendipity is written all over Modi's life. Although he became a *pracharak*, he would have also made a great soldier or a monk but could not, so that at the right time, he could be jettisoned into politics. He would have been stuck in the rut of Gujarat politics; had he not been banished to Delhi where he made priceless contacts in the party and others at the national level. Similarly, had the Gujarat riots occurred later in his career as the Chief Minister, when he was in full control, it could have proved to be a roadblock in his path to Prime Ministership.

His favourite Ganesha, whose many unique idols are his proud possession, was removing every obstacle which could have come in the way of his ultimate mission. 'Fortunate are the very few, like you, who are constantly blessed by Ganesha', someone with psychic abilities had once told Modi, in Gandhinagar. An umbrella of divine protection has always been over Narendra Modi. Gandhi too had this God's gift which inspired and impacted him, believes Modi.

It is interesting to compare the style of service and sacrifice of the Mahatma with that of Modi. Gandhi's father, prime minister of Porbandar, could afford to send his son to London to study law. Gandhi gave up a thriving legal practice in South Africa to become a servant of the masses. At 38, he took a vow of poverty and celibacy. After surrendering whatever property or money he had, he adopted poverty and started wearing a loincloth. Although a devout Hindu, Gandhi was greatly impressed by Jesus Christ and Christian ideas of nonviolence, forgiveness towards the enemy and passive moral resistance. Gandhi was the ultimate idealist. He never accepted public office and wanted to dissolve the Congress after Independence. He was more interested in showing the moral compass to the world, not to govern India.

Gandhi operated on a spiritual philosophical moral plane. He voluntarily embraced and glorified poverty. He was influenced by the philosophy of Tolstoy, Jainism, and Sermon on the Mount. Gandhi believed that it was only with the purity of poverty that one could come closer to the Truth and God. Post independence, Gandhi wanted India to go back to its villages where its soul lay and not be urbanized and industrialized. Nehru, the modernist, naturally disagreed with this stance. Ambedkar too criticized Gandhi for institutionalising poverty and ignoring structural problems, like caste oppression and inequality.

In the final years of his life, an anguished Gandhi became somewhat distanced from reality. He was compelled to use his favourite weapon of fast unto death, not only against the British, but against his own countrymen to make them see reason.

Gandhi's Mission was to secure independence with minimum loss of life. And set a high moral standard for the

Nation. He was never a pragmatist, and the moral fibre of the struggle was more important to him, than its ultimate success. He inspired his country to morally resist a colonial power without any violence of thought or action. However, when the Nation was experiencing the most traumatic birth throes, for those last few months of his life, his decisions became a trifle difficult to justify, causing anguish to all who loved him including Nehru and Patel.

Narendra Modi has unstinted admiration for the Mahatma's ability to instantly raise the consciousness of the masses. Modi recalls how by-the simple act of picking up a pinch of salt, Gandhiji sparked a nationwide movement of civil disobedience and resistance. In a speech given at Nagpur University, Modi had called Gandhi a great Communicator, which surprised a section of the audience who thought that the Mahatma was not such a great speaker. Modi went on to explain that Gandhi was not an orator, but he knew how to instantly connect with the consciousness of the masses, and that's why he was a great communicator. Modi, of course, is both an orator and a great communicator. During the COVID-19 crisis, the manner in which Modi convinced the entire nation including the Northeast to accept a Janata curfew preceding the lockdown, is evidence of this ability.

Narendra Modi has always had affinity for several Gandhian ideals like austerity, vegetarianism and use of Khadi.

On 2nd October 2003, which was the final day of the inaugural Vibrant Gujarat Global Investors' Summit, Modi took a personal initiative in organizing a Vegetarian Food Festival as also a unique Fashion Show at Gandhi's birthplace,

Porbandar. Students from the National Institute of Design and the National Institute of Fashion Technology walked the ramp as models wearing modern Khadi garments, to the tune of Gandhi's favourite bhajan '*Vaishnava jana to tene re kahiye*' (he who senses the pain of others). In conceptualising this Fashion Show, Modi sought the help of some experts in Gujarat who expressed their skepticism about such a fashion show ever being a success. Modi's confidence was however justified, when it proved to be a thundering hit with both global and Indian delegates. Later, Gandhian associates of Vinoba Bhave too praised Modi's approach by stating that 'if we want to make Khadi popular, this is the way forward'. Modi called it a 'courageous event' and stated that his objective was to ensure that Khadi goes beyond mere political symbolism and into everyday fashion.

Extolling the value of vegetarianism, Modi said at the Food Festival, that when you offer food grains to the Fire of Hunger (*jathragni*), you are performing a Yagna (sacred ritual by making offerings to the conse- crated fire); however, when food grains are substituted with flesh, the Fire turns into a *Chita* (crematoria fire). Murari Bapu, the world-renowned *Ramayana* narrator, complimented Modi for this original way of advocating vegetarianism.

The Mahatma too messaged in many original ways and was indeed a unique personage, feels Narendra Modi, who is fascinated by Gandhi's distinctive style like having a pocket watch dangling from his waist instead of a wrist watch; sitting with his knees tucked inwards instead of cross-legged; a Khadi sling bag worn diagonally across his chest instead of on one shoulder; using a wooden staff as a walking stick even when Gandhi was not infirm; steel-rimmed round glasses; carrying his mini eating kit wherever he went. Gandhi advocated swadeshi (boycott of foreign goods and using goods manufactured in India). Modi greatly emphasizes self-reliance.

Even earlier in life than the Mahatma, Narendra Modi gave up family life, matrimony, and whatever little money he had earned. When he became prime minister, he surrendered a valuable plot of land allotted to all legislators in Gujarat. He donated his savings from the salary as chief minister of Gujarat for 13 years, to a welfare fund for girl education. In order to be available 24/7, 365 days to the nation, he took no holidays. He made the ultimate sacrifice to the country, that is, of his entire lifetime.

However, unlike Gandhi, Modi has worked for a modern assertive India and its muscular national resurgence. He obviously does not believe in the philosophy of the Sermon on the Mount of offering his other cheek to the person who has unjustly slapped him.

In September 2025, as Modi turns 75 with eleven years as the prime minister, Modi's Mission is by no means complete. Narendra Modi continues to dream and has reserves of energy to implement those yet unfulfilled dreams. He dreams that in 2035, India's economy will reach USD 10 trillion and realistically be the world's second largest. In the Viksit Bharat vision of 2047, the stated objective is USD 30 trillion. Modi genuinely believes that India can achieve an 8% plus real growth rate. Under Make-in-India 2.0, India can grab supply chain exits from China, which, in a decade, may start to experience signs of internal strain. The national logistics policy plus Gati Shakti corridors can cut logistics cost to less than 6% of GDP. In 2014, it was 16% and is already down to 13%. Modi is determined to reach his obsessive target of zero import of fossil fuels, with solar, wind, ocean power, green hydrogen and battery giga parks. Possibly with those huge reserves of oil in the Andamans. The Employment Linked Incentive Scheme can generate 35 million jobs over a two years period. Skill India 2.0 will focus on AI, EVs, defence, semiconductors and robotics.

However, more than anything else, Narendra Modi aspires for India to be an egalitarian society. By 2035, he believes that the Direct Benefit Transfer system will include delivery to each underserved citizen of universal basic services like health, insurance, and education through vouchers. He is pushing for outcome-based fund transfers, which are tied to tangible learning and health metrics. And the cause dearest to his heart, of women welfare, wants to see half of the new net jobs going to women.

Zero tolerance for terrorism, both internal and cross-border, is already a policy of the Modi government with its forward deterrence doctrine. Modi loves to discuss with military technical experts about AI enabled fencing and detection methods. In the international arena, the aspiration is to have a permanent seat on the UN Security Council. Modi's laundry list is endless-defence modernisation and exports, leadership in space and technology. Modi is, of course, aware that some of these goals maybe delayed by fiscal constraints or human capital gaps or geopolitical crisis.

However, these goals will not be derailed.

What is Narendra Modi's vision for India, 50 years later, in 2075. He believes that in the entire world, India alone (unlike China, Europe and Japan), will have that rare combination of no demographic decline as well as accelerating growth. While most countries of the world will be experiencing a scary demographic decline, the Indian population growth will still be robust or at least not negative. The cumulative effect will be India emerging as a superpower with a strong possibility of being the world's largest economy. AI driven technology, quantum computing, green space, robotics and genomics will make Bharat the leader of all nations, is Narendra Modi's inner optimism.

5

In those quiet moments as a wintery Delhi dawn breaks out and he sips ginger tea, sitting alone wrapped in a red shawl, staring intently at the dew drop on a big leaf fluttering slightly in the ice-cold breeze, what thoughts pass through his mind. Does he think of his mother, the one person whom he loved unconditionally during her long and hard life of 99 years, and with whom he hardly spent anytime after he became Gujarat CM, barring her solitary brief visit to his official residence, after he became PM. Returning home at dusk with the family cow in Vadnagar after bathing her at the Sharmistha lake. About the affection and spiritual guidance, he received lifelong from the spiritual giants across the country.

The priceless mentoring of his Vakil Saheb during his

early years in the Sangh. Serving jaggery tea in tiny, chipped glasses at the Vadnagar railway platform to soldiers travelling to the battlefront. Suppressing tears of joy while kissing the threshold of the Lok Sabha when he entered Parliament for the first time. Meditating on the orange flames of a funeral pyre at the Manikarnika ghat during those youthful Himalayan wanderings. Prostrating before the smiling 5-year-old Ram Lalla idol in Ayodhya after performing the first *abhishek*. Cremating endless number of swollen bloated corpses after the dam burst in Morbi. Travelling coast to coast alone on a greyhound bus in America. Trying desperately to revive his hoarse voice with ginger and honey before the last election rally at Balia in UP on May 10, 2014. Of all those friends and colleagues who had stood by him, like a rock during adversity, also a few who had betrayed. The goose pimples he invariably feels while shouting Jai Hind or Bharat Mata ki Jai from the ramparts of the Red Fort. Those precious moments of his sadhana when he feels the fleeting presence of the Divine Mother. That great feeling of cleansing upon the successful completion of nine days of the Navratri fast with only warm water. The single unified connect he makes with a 100,000 strong rally during an emotional speech. The bliss occasionally experienced when his Higher Self steps out of the body and mind of Narendra Modi. And that constant humbling realisation that he is merely an instrument of the Cosmic programmed to perform obligations towards his country and his people.

The forces which govern India's destiny ought to be mighty pleased with Narendra Modi's performance. However, every soul is provided with a body and mind to maximize the purpose of his incarnation. So long as they are functioning robustly, any artificial age limit is irrelevant. Considering that Narendra Modi survives mostly on a diet of khichdi, steamed veggies and fruits, interspersed with periods of long fasting on warm water, from where he derives the energy to execute those insane daily domestic and foreign schedules, is a mystery. He says that his work ethic keeps him energized every moment.

Narendra Modi is grateful to the Cosmic for what he calls '*Avirat dhara*' (perennial flow) of newness, freshness and vitality, he experiences every living second. This is attributable only to a boon from God (*Ishwariya*), he feels. Be as it may, Modi's Mission has still to run its balance predestined course. Bharat Bhagya Bhawani expects nothing less from Narendra Damodardas Modi.

From his youth, Modi has never thought of himself as an individual with desires, feelings, or aspirations. He intuitively knew that he was chosen as an instrument to put India on the path of being a superpower. This was confirmed by his spiritual guides and a host of other saints whom he encountered during his personal spiritual journey. He has always been a stoic to whom joy or sadness matters not. Everyone like him who has long conquered the fear of death, is indifferent to whatever is to transpire in the future. What concerns him are national issues, and maybe to a limited extent, the issues of his party.

Narendra Modi has achieved his youthful dream, which he noted in his diary, in 1986, of lighting a lamp of hope in millions of feeble dreamless eyes. In the decades to come, future generations will find it difficult to believe that a single individual did so much and for so long for Bharat and its people.

Fifty years later, Modi and Gandhi will be mentioned in the same breath and in the same order.

Glossary

Aadi Jyotirlinga: The first Jyotirlinga (divine lingam of light).

Aakashwani: All-India Radio (government).

Abhishek: Ritualistic bathing or anointment of a deity with sacred substances.

Adivasi: Indigenous tribal communities of India.

Agnipariksha: Trial by fire; a life-altering challenge.

Agniveers: Recruits under India's Agnipath scheme for short-term military service.

Akhand Bharat: Undivided India.

Anushthan: Taking a vow/resolve before embarking upon a major religious or spiritual initiative.

Asmita: Pride, self-respect, or assertion of identity.

Bajra: A staple crop.

Bal Swayamsevak: RSS volunteer since childhood.

Bandh: A general strike or shutdown.

Bandi: Indian jacket.

Bapu: Father.

Benami: Property held by a person who is not the beneficial owner.

Beti Bachao, Beti Padhao: Save the girl child; educate the girl child.

Bhairava: A fearful form of Shiva; associated with guardianship/death.

Bharat Ratna: Jewel of India—India's highest civilian award.

Bharoto Bhagyo Vidhata: Dispenser of India's Destiny.

Bhashini: A digital platform developed by the Indian government to promote language accessibility.

Bhawani Bharati or Ma Bhawani Bharati: Mother India.

Bilipatra: Bilva leaf or Bael leaf (from the *Aegle marmelos* tree).

Biryani: A fragrant rice dish made with spices.

Brahmamoorat: Most sacred time of the day (3:30 to 4:30 a.m.) (Hindu).

Chappals: Flat, open-toe Indian sandals.

Churidar: Indian tight pants.

Dal: Indian lentil preparation, everyday staple food.

Dalda: A brand name which was synonymous with hydrogenated vegetable oil (vanaspati ghee).

Darshan: To view the image of God in a temple/or of a saint or sage.

Déjà vu: The feeling that one has experienced the same thing before.

Dharma: Righteous duty, moral order, or the cosmic law.

Dhotis: Loincloth wrapped around the waist, traditional Indian dress.

Ganesh Pooja: Worship of Lord Ganesha, the remover of obstacles.

Ganesha: The Hindu elephant-headed God of all auspicious beginnings.

Gayatri Mantra: Invocation to the Sun Goddess, Savitri/ Gayatri.

Ghat: A flight of steps leading to a riverbank, or a mountain pass.

Ghazals: Poetic form consisting of rhyming couplets and a refrain.

Ghee: Clarified butter.

Har Ghar Jal: Welfare scheme for household tap connections ('Every home shall have water').

Harijan: Term used by Gandhiji for Dalits (now considered outdated).

Jagat Janani: Divine Mother.

Jai Hind: Victory to India or Long live India.

Jan Dhan Yojana: A scheme of the Modi government to bring banking to the masses.

Jowar: Sorghum (a staple).

Jyotirlinga: A most sacred self-appearing object of Lord Shiva, Shivalinga in a temple (only 12 in India).

Kartik Poornima: Full moon day in the Hindu month of Kartik.

Khichdi: A rice dish, everyday diet.

Kho Kho: An Indian sport.

Kriya: A yogic or spiritual technique involving movement, breath, and focus.

Kshatriya: Warrior/ruler caste in Hindu tradition.

Kurta: Traditional Indian shirt.

Lakh: One hundred thousand.

Lalla: Lord Ram in child form.

Langars: Free temple food service.

Linga: Phallic symbol representing Shiva.

Mahamrityunjaya: Sacred protective potent Hindu mantra against illness/death.

Mahavidyas: Ten different forms of the Divine Female Force, wisdom goddesses.

Maryada Purushottam: A highly disciplined, optimal/ideal/perfect man.

MLA: Member of Legislative Assembly (state).

Modi Ghanchi: A caste in Gujarat, of oilseed pressers.

Mohollas: Narrow lane; street.

MP: Member of Parliament.

Mujahideen: Islamic fighter (literally 'one engaged in jihad').

Matths: Monastic institutions or spiritual centers in Hindu tradition.

Na khaoonga, na khaane doonga: I will not take bribes, nor will I allow others to take.

Navratri: Nine nights festival dedicated to the Goddess Durga.

NSSO: The National Sample Survey Office.

Om Gan Ganpataye Namah: A sacred potent mantra dedicated to Lord Ganesha.

Om Shree Ganeshaya Namah: Invoking Lord Ganesha (mantra).

Operation Parakrama: Indian massive military mobilisation post-2001 Parliament terrorist attack.

Param Vir Chakra: India's highest military honour awarded for the highest degree of valour in the presence of the enemy.

Pir: Muslim holy man; a saint.

Pitambara Devi: A Goddess, form of Durga.

Pracharak: Full-time worker of the RSS.

Pran-Pratishthan: Consecration (of idol).

Pucca: Permanent, well-constructed (usually referring to buildings or roads).

Rajdharma: Responsibility/duty of a King to be even-handed.

Ram Chabutra: Platform to mark Lord Rama's resting spot in Ayodhya.

Ram Lalla Virajman: Infant Lord Ram enthroned.

Rashtra: Nation or homeland.

Rath Yatra: A procession/march carrying an image of the deity.

Rotis: Indian bread; daily staple food (Hindi).

Sadhak: One who practices spiritual discipline.

Sadhana: Spiritual discipline.

Sadhu: Indian holy man.

Saheb: Sir (in Gujarati).

Sainik: Soldier.

Samadhi: A saint voluntarily surrendering his life.

Sanātana Dharma: Ancient Vedic Hindu religion/way of life.

Sangh: The RSS; Rashtriya Swayamsevak Sangh (abbr.).

Sangh Parivar: Organisations ideologically affiliated to the RSS.

Sangharsh ma Gujarat: *Gujarat in Struggle* (Memoirs of the Emergency period, a book in Gujarati written by Narendra Modi).

Shakha: A branch.

Shakti: Female Divine Power.

Tantra: Esoteric spiritual system involving ritua
and energy work.

Thali: A traditional Indian plate (vessel) in which a
served.

Tilak: Mark on the forehead signifying devotion, cast
spiritual identity.

Treta Yuga: Ancient Vedic period in history.

Ugra Swaroop: Stern form.

Upaasak: Practitioner of spiritual disciplines.

Vaaksiddhi: Whatever a person says materializes, transpires, or ultimately comes to pass (a spiritual attainment).

Vallabham Gajananam Ek Dantam: A powerful mantra invoking Ganesha.

Vanaspati: Hydrogenated vegetable edible oil.

Vanvaas: Forest exile.

Viksit Bharat: Developed India.

Yagna: An elaborate Vedic ceremony to cleanse, propitiate, worship.

Zamindari: Feudal landholding system during Mughals and British India.